THE FUTURE OF GOLD

THE MACMILLAN COMPANY
NEW YORK · BOSTON · CHICAGO · DALLAS
ATLANTA · SAN FRANCISCO

MACMILLAN & CO., LIMITED
LONDON · BOMBAY · CALCUTTA
MELBOURNE

THE MACMILLAN COMPANY
OF CANADA, LIMITED
TORONTO

THE FUTURE OF GOLD

BY

PAUL EINZIG

NEW YORK

THE MACMILLAN COMPANY

1935

Printed in the United States of America

PREFACE

IN writing this book the author has pursued a fourfold object. He has endeavoured to forecast as far as possible the course the London price of gold is likely to follow in the near future and in the more distant future. He has also attempted to arrive at a conclusion about the level at which sterling and the other principal currencies are likely to be eventually stabilised. Thirdly, he has tried to make up his mind what type of monetary system the leading countries are likely to adopt when returning to stability. Lastly, he has aimed at forming an opinion about the tendency of gold and commodity prices after the stabilisation of currencies. None of these tasks are easy, since complete uncertainty prevails about the intentions of the various Governments, and about the tendency of various major factors.

The author hastens to make it plain that it is not his ambition to compete with *Old Moore's Almanac* by foretelling what the price of gold will be on February 17 or on August 9 next. It is humanly impossible to do more than enumerate the factors that are likely to affect the price of gold and to express a considered opinion as to the likelihood of their appearance and the effect of their operations. The author is not in a position to foretell for certain whether a given event—such as, for instance, the devaluation of the franc—will or will not take place, much less when exactly that event will occur. His aim is merely to state how a particular event, if and when it materialises, will affect the price of gold.

Considering the extent of misunderstanding and the number of popular fallacies that exist, the author is convinced that there is scope for providing such a guide for the maze of the gold problem. To give only one example of the confusion of thought that prevails: It is a popular belief that, were France to devalue the franc, the appreciation of sterling in terms of francs would be accompanied by a corresponding fall in the London price of gold. Whether or not France devalues the franc remains to be seen, but it is advisable to know that, if and when she does so, it will not cause a fall in the London price of gold. Another popular error is that if after stabilisation there should be a glut of gold, the result would be a fall in the price of the metal. The author maintains that, whether or not there will be a glut of gold is a matter of opinion. It is a fact, however, that even a glut of gold would be unable to affect its market price once the currencies are stabilised.

Those who have made a study of the gold problem can be divided, generally speaking, into two classes: theoretical economists who are not acquainted with the practical side of the problem, and practical specialists who do not possess an adequate theoretical background to view the problem from a broad perspective. The author assumes a position half-way between the theoretical economist and the practical specialist, and has endeavoured in this book to combine the abstract and concrete viewpoints. In his daily "Lombard Street" column appearing in the *Financial News*, he has followed for many years the theoretical and practical aspects of the gold problem; those who have followed his column regularly may find some of his arguments familiar, but by far the greater part of the book contains material hitherto unpublished.

From the point of view of their attitude towards the problem, most of those who have dealt with it in the past belong either to the group of orthodox economists and bankers or to that of radical currency reformers. Both groups approach the problem with very definite preconceived ideas. As the author belongs to no group, he feels he has the right to claim to be less prejudiced than either those who advocate the return of the system exactly as it operated in the past, or those who demand that the gold standard should be abolished altogether. In the author's opinion, there is nothing fundamentally wrong with the gold standard; indeed, if there were no such system it ought to be invented. On the other hand he considers it simply unthinkable that this country should ever return to the state of affairs when a small loss of gold necessitated a high bank rate and credit restrictions which victimised hundreds of thousands of wage-earners. He believes that the gold standard failed in 1931 mainly, if not exclusively, on account of the lack of adequate gold supplies. In his opinion, the remedy lies in a drastic devaluation of sterling and other currencies, which would create a margin of gold reserve sufficient to enable the authorities to manage the monetary policy of their countries from the broader point of view of producers' and consumers' interests, instead of being at the mercy of fluctuations in their gold stocks. He is convinced that devaluation would not be followed by a sufficiently substantial rise in commodity prices to wipe out the book-keeping surplus of gold reserve thereby created.

The object of this book is essentially to serve as a guide for the man in the street. The author has endeavoured to eliminate as far as possible technicalities and abstract questions, these being dealt with in the Appendices. Those concerned mainly with the near future will find that subject dealt with in Chapters III. to VI.; those interested in the prospects of definite stabilisation will find answers to their many doubts and queries in Chapters VII. to IX. The prospects of gold after stabilisation are examined in Chapters X. and XI., while the last chapter is devoted to the examination of various factors, other than the price, affecting gold mining shares. In Chapter II. the reader will find a list of "bear points" and "bull points" that are likely to affect gold and gold-mining shares. In the Summary following Chapter XII. the likely short-term and long-term effects of the various factors are indicated in tabular form.

THE WHITE COTTAGE,
SOUTH BOLTON GARDENS,
LONDON, S.W., *October* 1934

P. E.

CONTENTS

CHAPTER I

INTRODUCTORY

Popular interest in the future of gold is of recent origin. Until 1931, when Great Britain departed from the gold standard, the man in the street was entirely indifferent towards the discussions that took place amongst experts on the gold problem. Even during and after the war, the British public regarded the abnormal conditions affecting gold as essentially temporary, and took it for granted that sooner or later the *status quo* would be restored. It was assumed that the restoration of the gold standard in most civilised countries, and the decline in the London market price of gold to its pre-war level, were a mere question of time. After 1925, events appeared to have proved this assumption to be correct. As a result, after the stabilisation of sterling, nobody, apart from a small number of economists, took any interest in the controversies about the wisdom of maintaining the gold standard and about the prospects of changes in the commodity value of gold. Business men, investors, wage-earners, and the rest of the mixed company covered by the vague term of "general public", regarded these questions as belonging to the realm of metaphysics, and left them to the specialists.

Since 1931, the man in the street can no longer afford to maintain his attitude of indifference towards the gold problem. The suspension of the gold standard in Great Britain and a number of other countries has thrown the whole monetary system into the melting-pot. The restoration of the conditions prevailing before the crisis can no longer be regarded as a mere question of time. Indeed, apart from a small and diminishing group of orthodox economists, nobody seriously believes that the system, in the form in which it existed before 1931, will ever be restored; and not even the most orthodox deflationists dare to hope that the London price of gold will ever be reduced to its old figure. The question of the future of gold has assumed immense practical importance, and the public feels itself reluctantly compelled to take an interest in it.

Three major questions, or rather, sets of questions, arise from the speculation about the future of gold. They are:

(1) What will be the future trend of the price of gold, and at what level will it be stabilised?

(2) Will the gold standard be restored, and if so, in what form?

(3) Will there be a glut or a scarcity of gold after the stabilisation of currencies?

The reason why it is so difficult to provide a reliable answer to these questions is that, amidst the uncertainty prevailing in regard to the international monetary situation, there are hardly any "fixed points" on which inferences can safely be based.

While until 1931 the continued existence of the institution of the gold standard was taken for granted, during the last three years a strong current of opinion has developed favouring the abolition of this system. It has become customary to put the blame for all the world's troubles upon the gold standard, which has thus become a most unpopular institution. The number of those who advocate the demonetisation of gold has increased considerably; others do not go so far, and merely suggest admitting silver into partnership on an equal footing with gold as the basis of the monetary system. Others, again, believe in retaining gold as the sole monetary metal, but advocate the restriction of its functions. These movements have inevitably created an unsettled feeling in the minds of those concerned with the future of gold.

The question whether any of the before-mentioned proposals is likely to materialise and, if so, how it would affect the price of gold, has assumed considerable practical importance. In any case, apart altogether from these doubts, the future of gold has also become obscured by the uncertainty as to the fluctuation of sterling, and the rate at which it will eventually be stabilised. President Roosevelt's unstable and ever-changing policy has introduced yet another unknown factor into the gold situation and outlook. Uncertainty as to the fate of the franc and other gold currencies adds to the difficulties of the task of forming a definite opinion about the prospects of gold.

For the past two years or so it has been pointed out by a number of experts and pseudo-experts that the ruling price of gold is too high, and that, even though it may temporarily rise further, it must eventually decline to a lower level. This prophecy is mostly a case of the wish being father to the thought. Radical would-be reformers advocating the abolition of the gold standard like to think that their proposals will eventually materialise, and their faith in their ultimate success explains their forecast of a slump in the price of gold. At the other extreme, orthodox economists are equally emphatic in predicting a fall in the price of gold on the ground that, in the present circumstances, the supply of monetary gold is likely to be well in excess of what they consider normal and natural monetary demand. The two extremes thus meet in their firm belief in the coming gold slump.

The problem is of first-rate importance from more than one point of view. Apart from the general interest it represents to every section of the community on account of its bearing on monetary developments, it is of practical importance to a large number of people directly concerned with gold. The number of those who own gold mining shares has increased considerably during the last three years—it probably now runs well into six figures. In addition, many thousands of people all over the world have acquired gold to safeguard themselves against the risks attached to the holding of any other forms of investment. All these investors follow with keen interest the controversy over the prospects of gold. Last, but by no means least, the problem of the future of gold has political aspects which should not be ignored.

In order to avoid confusion of thought, it is essential to define the issue at stake. An endless source of confusion is due to lack of discrimination between the "price" of gold and the "value" of gold. Another rich source of error is inadequate realisation of the difference between the short view and the long view. By "price" of gold we mean its London market price expressed in terms of sterling—an essentially accurate and easily defined term. By "value" of gold we mean its purchasing power determined by the level of prices, which is an essentially abstract, theoretical, and vague notion. Throughout this book we shall be concerned with the "price" of gold, although we cannot ignore the question of movements in the price-level. It is of equal importance to discriminate between the short view and the long view taken about the prospects of gold. In this book we are mainly concerned with the long view; that is to say, the level at which gold will settle down eventually after the stabilisation of the principal currencies. It is this view that matters the most, both from the standpoint of economists and of investors. At the same time, the factors affecting the temporary fluctuations of gold, pending its definite stabilisation, are also of importance, both from the general point of view of the economist and from the practical point of view of the investor. Indeed, it is these fluctuations that are likely to influence to a high degree the final choice of the rates of stabilisation.

In order to be able to form an opinion about the price of gold in the near future it is necessary to examine the factors affecting the exchange rate of sterling. After all, the London market price of gold depends—so long as there is at least one other currency on a gold basis—almost exclusively upon the international value of sterling. If the Bank of France or the American monetary authorities are prepared to buy and sell gold at a fixed price, then the London price of gold expressed in sterling cannot materially depart from the sterling equivalent of the official franc or dollar price of gold. It is therefore necessary for our purpose to consider the likelihood of an appreciation or a depreciation of sterling. This in itself is a highly complicated subject, as the prospects of sterling are determined by a large number of known and unknown factors. The trade balance, the international movement of funds to and from London, the policy of the Exchange Equalisation Fund, the general monetary policy of the authorities, the attitude of speculators: these are some of the factors in question. The tendency of the two other principal currencies—the dollar and the franc—is also likely to influence sterling, and hence the London price of gold, to a large extent. The question of a further devaluation of the dollar by President Roosevelt is of primary importance, as is also the attitude of France towards devaluation. Again, another set of factors is represented by the attitude of those engaged in hoarding gold, although it must be emphasised that the extent of hoarding or of dishoarding only affects the premium of gold on the franc and the dollar.

Many other factors may result in wide movements of a temporary character in the price of gold. The majority of those who hold either gold or gold shares, however, consider such fluctuations to be of minor importance, for they have acquired their holdings in the belief that by this means they will, in the long run, be safeguarded from capital depreciation. So long as they are satisfied that, taking a long view, they are safe, they can afford to ignore any provisional upward or downward movements. While a large section of investors acquired its holdings for speculative purposes in order to take advantage of any temporary rise and to get in and out of the market in accordance with the movement of the price, it is to be assumed that the predominant majority is not affected by such considerations. All that the latter want is to be on the safe side, and to that end they are prepared to forgo, not only speculative profit obtained through a quick capital appreciation, but even an adequate yield on their investment. In the opinion of these investors, it is only the long view that matters. It is incomparably safer for this class of investor to rely upon the logic of arguments than it is for those who seek to make profit through the intelligent anticipation of temporary movements.

To predict what the approximate price of gold is likely to be three months or six months hence is bordering on the impossible. It is much easier to make a forecast as to the level at which gold will eventually settle down. To that end, it is necessary to consider not only the factors that are likely to affect the price of gold, but also the chances of any fundamental change in the monetary system. Is it reasonable to assume that gold will be abandoned definitely by a number of important countries ? Is it probable that its monetary use will be limited either through the adoption of a system of managed currencies in which gold would play only a subsidiary part, or through the adoption of bimetallism ? Will the Central Banks in the leading countries be under statutory obligation to buy gold at a fixed price? These are only some of the questions selected, at random, to give an idea of the range of problems to be dealt with.

Hitherto we have been dealing with the question of the price of gold. The commodity value of gold matters little in the short run, though it may become a factor of importance in the long run. It is determined by the tendency in the price level. From the point of view of investors, a situation may conceivably arise in which the advantage of a rise in the sterling price of gold may be offset by a fall in its commodity value. If the same amount of gold buys fewer commodities in three years' time than it does now, then the endeavour to preserve the value of capital by investing it in gold or gold mining shares has failed fully to achieve its object. Is there any likelihood of such a situation arising again? Is there, again, a likelihood of a rise in the cost of production sufficient to offset the beneficial effect of the rise in the sterling price of gold? Such questions are of great practical importance, and any views on the future of gold cannot be complete without dealing with them.

CHAPTER II

GOLD AS AN INVESTMENT

INVESTORS who hold gold or gold mining shares are concerned not only with the tendencies affecting the value of gold before the stabilisation of currencies, but also with the circumstances of their stabilisation, which will, in the long-run, determine the value of their investment.

During the period of comparative stability that preceded the war, investment was a simple matter. So long as the investor was satisfied with a relatively low yield, it was easy for him to avoid speculative risks. Since the war, and more particularly since the crisis, things have become much more complicated for the investor. While, in the olden days, anyone who was prepared to accept a low yield could secure for himself peace of mind, to-day a low yield, or even the complete absence of yield, is no safeguard against the danger of capital depreciation. Amidst the present unsettled conditions almost anything may happen and even the most conservative trustee securities carry with them a certain risk.

Before 1914 Government stocks were considered the highest form of security. During the past twenty years, however, the fall of currencies and international defaults have inflicted heavy losses upon holders of Government securities in many countries. Holders of British Government securities have escaped such losses, although they were affected by the low price of

Government securities during and after the war, and also by the increase in the cost of living, which reduced the commodity value of gilt-edged stocks. As regards the future of British Government securities, while a default is unthinkable (unless an extreme Socialistic Government comes into power), it is conceivable that a drastic devaluation of the pound might inflict losses upon holders. For this reason, a large number of conservative investors, who, in the past, would never have thought of departing from trustee stocks, endeavour to invest their money in some other form which safeguards them against loss through a depreciation of sterling. It is obviously useless to send capital abroad for that purpose; the chances are that other currencies will also depreciate, many of them to a higher degree than sterling.

Real estate is one of the favourite forms of "safety first" investment, but there are two reasons why many investors are reluctant to commit themselves too much in that direction. The one is that, in the eventuality of a Socialist Government being returned, real estate is the form of property likely to be the hardest hit by unchecked taxation, and the most difficult to dispose of. The other reason is that real property is usually very slow in adjusting itself to the new value of a currency. Whenever a currency depreciates, wholesale prices adjust themselves to the new level within a few years. Retail prices, the cost of living, and wages are slower to adjust themselves, while the price of real property usually lags many years behind in the process of adjustment.

Many investors hope to safeguard themselves against currency depreciation by holding industrial shares, for, if the depreciation remains moderate, such shares are likely, on the whole, to rise sufficiently to compensate investors for the depreciation of the currency. The difficulty lies in the choice of the right type of industrial share. The prosperity of an industrial enterprise depends upon so many unforeseen considerations that the holding of shares inevitably involves a high degree of speculative risk which many investors are anxious to avoid.

A large and increasing number of people believe they have discovered the obvious solution, which is to acquire gold, or gold mining shares. The British public is not at all keen on hoarding gold, but abroad it is easily the most popular form of "safety first" investment. Englishmen have never acquired the hoarding habit, and even the uncertainty created by the crisis has failed to induce them to follow the foreign example. Instead of this, gold mining shares have become a favourite form of investment among a class of investors which, until recently, would have considered them too speculative. It stands to reason that gold mining shares should benefit by an appreciation of gold. As investments they possess several advantages over the holding of the actual metal. They yield a dividend, while the hoarding of gold involves expenses. Holders of gold shares need not be worried about any possibility of the Government threatening to confiscate their holding at a low price. On the other hand, holders of gold mining shares are exposed to higher taxation and to the speculative risk attached to every kind of mining enterprise.

Neither the holding of gold shares nor the holding of gold itself is without considerable disadvantages. They have become none the less a popular form of investment to safeguard against capital loss through currency depreciation. The question arises whether gold and gold mining shares really fulfil this requirement. In this respect expert opinion is by no means unanimous. From time to time holders are warned that, at their present price, gold or gold mining shares are over-valued; that, for various reasons, they are likely to fall considerably; or, at any rate, that a level has been reached at which the holding of gold or gold shares involves a high degree of risk.

The factors which affect the value of gold and of gold shares are complicated in the extreme. The investor, in order to be able to form an opinion whether the pessimistic forecasts are justified, would have to unite in himself the qualities of the economist, the foreign exchange expert, and the student of human nature.

We propose to give below a list of the most frequently quoted bull points and bear points for both gold and gold mining shares in general.

I. *Bear Points for Gold*

1. Sterling may appreciate (*a*) through seasonal demand; (*b*) through an influx of foreign funds; (*c*) through an improvement in the trade balance of Great Britain.
2. Holders of gold may dishoard on a large scale.
3. All countries, or most of them, may definitely abandon the gold standard.
4. They may adopt a restricted form of gold standard.
5. The rate of stabilisation may be fixed below the present level.
6. The rate of stabilisation may be lowered subsequently, as a result of a "gold inflation".

II. *Bull Points for Gold*

1. Sterling may further depreciate (*a*) through seasonal pressure ; (*b*) through an adverse trade balance ; (*c*) through overlending abroad; (*d*) through the withdrawal of foreign balances.
2. The gold contents of the dollar may be lowered further and sterling may be adjusted to the lower level.
3. The suspension of the gold standard in France may lead to a currency depreciation race.
4. There may be an increased demand for hoarding.
5. The rate of stabilisation may be fixed above the present level.

Most of these points concern the short view on gold. But in the long view, it is the final rate of stabilisation that matters the most.

III. *Bear Points for Gold Mining Shares*

1. The price of gold may fall.
2. The demand for gold may decline (*a*) through the adoption of bimetallism; (*b*) through the adoption of a managed currency; (*c*) through the adoption of a limited gold standard; (*d*) through a restriction of foreign trade; (*e*) through a restriction in the international transfer of funds.
3. The demand for gold may remain low through the maintenance of a low price-level.
4. Gold production may unduly increase.
5. Hoarding may cease.
6. The cost of production may increase.
7. Taxation on gold mines may increase.

The first of these points covers the whole range of

causes through which the price of gold may conceivably decline. The points relating to hoarding, production, cost of production, and taxation affect the short view on gold or gold mining shares, while the rest concern the long view.

IV. *Bull Points for Gold Mining Shares*

1. The price of gold may rise.
2. Central banks may want larger stocks than before the crisis.
3. Political and economic uncertainty may lead to further hoarding.
4. The price-level may rise.
5. The cost of production may not rise too rapidly.
6. Taxation may be reduced.

Here again, the first point covers the whole range of causes on account of which the price of gold may rise in the short or in the long run. Most of the remaining points concern mainly or exclusively the long view on gold mining shares.

We propose to examine in detail, in the following chapters, all these bear points and bull points for gold and gold mining shares. Although the answer to many questions lies in the realm of speculation, in most cases it is possible to arrive at a conclusion on the basis of a balance of probabilities. In some cases the degree of probability is very high. By accepting certain bear points or bull points as probable and eliminating others, the task of forming an opinion as to the prospects may be simplified to no slight degree.

CHAPTER III

GOLD AND STERLING

The price of gold in the London market is determined by the exchange rate of sterling in relation to the currencies based on gold. Factors of minor importance also influence the market price to some slight degree. The fluctuation of supply and demand affects the premium of gold on the gold exchanges, while the fluctuation of the franc-dollar exchange rate has also some slight influence. The range of these fluctuations is, however, rather less than 1 per cent of the London price of gold. Since the purpose of our enquiry is to form an opinion on the broad tendency likely to be followed by the price of gold, the minor factors which affect the premium of gold on the gold currencies, but not its basic price, may safely be disregarded. Our present task is confined to making a forecast of the probable movements of sterling in the near and the more distant future—a task by no means easy. In the foreign exchange market, as in war and in love, very frequently it is the unexpected that happens; unforeseen factors are often of fundamental importance. In this chapter we are concerned only with those factors which have direct bearing on the inherent strength or weakness of sterling, leaving factors that affect sterling indirectly through their influence on the dollar or the franc for the next two chapters.

It is, of course, very difficult to draw the line between factors affecting sterling directly and those affecting it through their effect on the dollar or the franc. When, for instance, the sterling-dollar rate rises, it is sometimes difficult to know for certain whether the movement is due to the strength of sterling or to the weakness of the dollar. There are, however, a number of factors which obviously affect directly the exchange position of this country. It is to these that we propose to confine ourselves in the present chapter. We shall endeavour to examine the prospects of sterling, assuming, for the sake of argument, that there will be no material change in the situation in the United States or in France.

Taking a short view, the seasonal movement of sterling cannot be disregarded among the factors affecting the price of gold. Throughout all the changes and developments in the situation, the seasonal fluctuations of sterling recur regularly. Every autumn sterling tends to depreciate as a result of heavy imports, and during the first quarter of the year it usually recovers through the improvement of the trade balance. This was so before the war and after the war, during the period of stability and also during the crisis. The extent of the seasonal depreciation varies, of course, widely and so do the dates when it begins and ends. At the time of writing, we are in the middle of a spell of seasonal weakness of sterling, and the chances are that, unless some outside factor intervenes, this seasonal movement will continue for some time. This means that, during that period, the London market price of gold will continue to rise. The probability is that, other things being equal, sterling will begin to recover towards the end of the year, and will accentuate its appreciation early in 1935. Consequently, in the natural course of events, the present rise in gold will reach its climax some time in the near future, and will be followed by a comparatively moderate set-back on account of the seasonal appreciation of sterling.

Taking the long view, the seasonal fluctuations of sterling are of no importance from the point of view of the trend of the price of gold. The general tendency of the trade balance is of far greater importance. Here again, the situation has remained substantially the same as it was before the war. Although post-war economic literature is wont to minimise the influence of the trade balance as a factor affecting the exchange, in reality it is of considerable importance even in the changed conditions. Whenever a currency is persistently weak, more often than not the figures of the trade balance of the country concerned provide the explanation. The weakness of sterling during the greater part of 1934 is explained, in part at any rate, by the adverse change in the trade balance compared with 1933. In addition to the increase of our import surplus, there was also a decline in our invisible exports. The yield from British overseas investments declined through default by Germany and a number of other countries. Moreover, for the first time since the beginning of the crisis, English people were once more travelling abroad in large numbers, thereby increasing our invisible imports. It is thus reasonable to assume that the trade balance of Great Britain during the current year compares more unfavourably with that of 1933 than would appear from the figures of visible trade alone.

This deterioration of the trade balance was due to the increase of imports, caused by the internal trade revival. It is difficult to say whether this revival will continue, and whether export trade will be able to keep pace with it. One thing is, however, certain. The favourable effect of the depreciation of sterling on the trade balance has diminished considerably owing to the depreciation of the dollar and the yen and the fall of prices and the adoption of tariffs and quotas abroad. Even though a further depreciation of sterling would help exports, the effect of this factor on the trade balance would be minimised by the watertight defence of home markets by quotas and other means.

From the figures of our balance of payments, it is evident that Great Britain cannot afford to lend abroad. There is no surplus available for that purpose. If, in spite of this, loans and credits are granted to various foreign countries, the result is further depreciation of sterling through overlending. Although there is at present an official embargo on foreign lending, exceptions are made in certain cases. There is, for instance, no objection to the issue of Colonial loans, which tend to affect sterling in a similar way as foreign loans, even though perhaps to a lesser degree. According to a recent statement made by the Chancellor of the Exchequer, exceptions will also be made in favour of loans to countries belonging to the Sterling Bloc, provided that the proceeds are used for the purpose of maintaining the stability of their currencies in relation to sterling; and also in favour of loans raised for the purpose of buying commodities in this country. In theory, such loans do not tend to depreciate sterling. In practice, however, the chances are that they will increase the selling pressure on it. Though a country of the Sterling Bloc may contract a loan in order to increase the sterling reserve of its Central

Bank, it does not necessarily follow that the balance thus created will be retained for ever. The Central Bank concerned may find it necessary to sell the sterling in order to support its currency. Again, in the case of loans granted for the purpose of financing foreign orders to British industries, the usual procedure is for part of the loan to be granted in cash, so as to enable the borrower to complete the work for which purpose the loan is contracted. British firms are very anxious to increase their sales abroad, and the Government is equally anxious to support them. The chances are, therefore, that the British authorities will not veto foreign loans partly granted in cash. This was the case in the recent transaction between the Polish Government and the Westinghouse Company. The latter supplied the material required for the Polish State Railways, but the total amount of the loan granted in connection with this transaction was several times larger than the amount spent on British goods. The cash portion of such transactions inevitably increases the selling pressure on sterling.

There can be no doubt, therefore, that on a modest scale, Great Britain is overlending. The granting of loans overseas on a small scale is likely to continue, for London cannot altogether relinquish her rôle of the world's banker. In addition, there is proceeding a certain amount of repatriation of British securities formerly held abroad. Two outstanding examples of such transactions are the repatriation of Boots and Enos shareholdings from the United States. All these capital items in the balance of payments tend to depreciate sterling. On the other hand, there is undoubtedly a certain amount of debt repayment going on. Although many foreign debtors suspended the sinking fund, some of them continue to make annual repayments. The Dominions are also likely to repay part of their debt contracted in London. Having accumulated huge sterling balances with which they do not know what to do, Australia, South Africa, and New Zealand will probably reduce their outstanding indebtedness to this country. In this case, however, the transactions will not involve any new purchase of sterling. On balance, long-term capital transactions are likely to work against sterling and consequently in favour of the gold price.

A very important capital item in the balance of payments is the movement of short-term funds. During the second and third quarters of 1934 the weakness of sterling was largely the result of the repatriation of French and other Continental balances from London. This movement was in part counteracted by the increase of American sterling balances. The present amount of foreign holdings of sterling must be quite considerable in spite of withdrawals during 1934.

Overseas balances may be divided into five categories. There are, in the first place, London balances of Dominions and Colonies. These are the most unlikely to leave London. In the normal course they will tend to increase rather than decline, since the exchange is in favour of some of the Dominions. The only possible reduction in these balances likely to occur would be through the repayment of Dominion loans. The second category of foreign balances includes those held by countries of the Sterling Bloc. These are also comparatively steady. As the fluctuation of sterling does not alter the value of these balances in terms of the currencies of the Sterling Bloc, there is no very strong incentive for those countries to increase or reduce their balances when sterling appreciates or depreciates. A steady depreciation of sterling might induce some of the Central Banks of the Sterling Bloc to convert their sterling reserve into gold. The third category of foreign holders of sterling balances includes the United States and countries whose currencies move in sympathy with the dollar. These balances are much less stable than those in the first two categories. Should President Roosevelt decide upon a definite stabilisation of the dollar, the greater part of these funds would be repatriated. Ruling out this possibility, the chances are that these balances will increase rather than decline. The fourth category of foreign balances includes those of the countries of the Gold Bloc. Most of these balances have been repatriated during the second and third quarters of 1934 as a result of the return of confidence in the stability of the franc. The chances are that, while sterling continues to depreciate through seasonal pressure, this process of repatriation will continue, but as soon as sterling begins to recover, some of the withdrawn funds will begin to find their way back to London. This movement is likely to assume immense proportions if and when there is a flight from the franc or from other currencies. We shall deal with that question in a subsequent chapter. There is also a fifth category of foreign balances, consisting of funds sent to London from Central European and other unstable countries. Generally speaking, these funds follow the tendency of the balances owned by countries of the Gold Bloc.

The probability is that the movements of short-term funds will be against sterling in the immediate future, but will turn strongly in favour of sterling before very long. Consequently, while at present this factor may contribute towards a further rise in the price of gold, before long it will most probably accentuate a relapse. The extent to which this factor will operate both ways will depend, of course, upon the attitude of the Exchange Equalisation Account.

Ever since its establishment, the Exchange Equalisation Account has endeavoured to mitigate the effect on sterling of the movements of foreign funds to and from London. During the second and third quarters of 1934 it sold at least £50 to £60 million of its gold stock in order to moderate the depreciation of sterling through the withdrawal of foreign funds. It appears probable that, when the tide turns, the official policy will again aim at preventing a sharp appreciation of sterling. Judging by past experience, the authorities will not resist rigidly an upward movement, but will mitigate it and delay it to a great extent.

Taking the long view, it seems reasonable to assume that the activities of the Exchange Equalisation Account tend to cause a depreciation of sterling. From the point of view of results, it is immaterial whether this is due to a deliberate policy, or merely to the necessity created by the course of events. Although the British authorities have never taken any deliberate action to cause sterling to depreciate, the activities of the Exchange Equalisation Account, none the less, produce that result. During the first quarter of 1932, the authorities bought a large amount of francs and dollars in order to prevent an unwanted appreciation of sterling. Later in the year the Exchange Equalisation Account re-sold part, but not the whole, of these francs and dollars in order to prevent an unwanted depreciation of sterling. They did not re-sell the whole amount bought, because a large part of it was used for the repayment of the outstanding balance of the Franco-American credits of £130 million contracted in 1931. Had the whole amount of francs and dollars bought earlier in the year been re-sold, sterling would have remained at a high level. As it was it depreciated to a new low record at the end of 1932.

Again in 1933, large amounts of gold were acquired by the Exchange Equalisation Account in order to prevent an unwanted appreciation of sterling. Later in the year, part, but not the whole, of this amount was re-sold, in order to prevent an unwanted depreciation of sterling. Some £60 million of the gold acquired earlier in the year was sold to the Bank of England and added to the latter's gold reserve. The net result of the above policy was again a tendency for sterling to depreciate to new low records. In 1934 there was no visible evidence of the same tactics. Gold was bought freely during the first quarter and it was re-sold freely during the second and third quarters of the year. It may be reasonably assumed, however, that in August 1934, when the Exchange Equalisation Account practically ceased to support sterling, it still held a substantial gold stock which it had meant to retain.

The pursuance of such tactics will result in an accumulation of a substantial gold reserve. If the Exchange Equalisation Account buys gold every time sterling is strong and re-sells only part of this gold every time sterling is weak, then in the long-run its gold stock will increase considerably; but at the same time sterling is bound to depreciate. Those who are inclined to criticise this policy should be reminded that this is the only way in which our authorities can possibly accumulate a sufficiently large gold reserve to enable them to stabilise sterling without taking undue risk. The necessity for increasing the gold reserve before stabilising is certainly a most important bear point for sterling, and a most important bull point for gold. This factor, which is often overlooked, outweighs in importance all other factors having a direct bearing on sterling.

The general economic policy and the monetary policy pursued by the British Government are also such as to tend to cause a depreciation of sterling in the long run. It is highly probable that this country will swim with the tide regarding the increase of customs and tariffs and other restrictions to imports. All such measures tend to cause a rise in commodity prices. The policy of cheap money pursued by the Government works in the same direction. It is true that the British Government has so far avoided embarking upon any expensive public works schemes, such as would stimulate a rise in prices. Notwithstanding this, its economic and monetary policy tends to work in the same direction. Its action in restoring cuts in salaries and unemployment relief also tends to produce a similar result, as it is likely to lead to an all-round increase of wages and salaries. Some progress has, in fact, been made already in this direction, with a resultant general increase in the cost of production and the price-level. This again means that the economic parities of sterling are adjusting themselves to a large extent to its depreciated exchange value. In doing so they tend to create a permanent justification for its depreciation. This factor also works towards a depreciation of sterling and a rise in the sterling price of gold in the long run. The effect of rising prices in the United States on the value of sterling will be dealt with in the next chapter.

Last, but perhaps not least, there are some political factors which also tend to cause sterling to depreciate. Considerations of Imperial policy would make a depreciation of sterling desirable. As is well known, the exchanges of Australia and New Zealand are at a 25 per cent discount in relation to sterling. For the sake of Imperial economic unity it would be desirable to restore them to parity. This end could be attained either through an appreciation of the Australian and New Zealand pounds to the level of sterling, or by a depreciation of sterling to the level of the Australian and New Zealand pounds. It is most unlikely that the two Dominions would be prepared to deflate for the sake of Imperial economic unity. The only way, therefore, to attain that end would be for this country to depreciate its currency sufficiently to enable the Dominions to restore theirs to power without having to deflate to that end.

A much more important consideration is that political stability in India necessitates a rising tendency of the price-level. It is thanks to the prosperity caused by the depreciation of the rupee, which is linked to sterling, that political discontent in India has declined during the last three years. It is not likely that the British Government would deliberately reverse this factor, and expose itself to the political consequences of new deflationary depression in India.

The factor of home policy also most definitely tends towards a further depreciation of sterling. As the next General Election will be held some time during 1935 or 1936, the National Government cannot afford to antagonise the electorate by pursuing a monetary policy causing an accentuation of the economic depression. On the contrary, it will have to do its utmost to assist the revival. Although such considerations do not play as important a part in this country as they do in the United States, they cannot be omitted from the list of factors affecting sterling. It is the approach of the General Election which makes it improbable that the Government will decide to stabilise sterling in the near future.

A much more important factor is the anticipation of a Socialist victory at the next General Election. It is certain that the advent of a Socialist Government would be accompanied by a wholesale flight of capital from Britain, and a consequent slump of sterling. With the approach of the General Election a large number of people are likely to anticipate such a development, and take timely steps to be on the safe side. Large amounts of capital are likely to be transferred abroad and invested in Wall Street or in other markets. This factor in itself would be sufficient to cause sterling to depreciate a few months before the General Election.

It is, therefore, safe to conclude that, if nothing spectacular happens abroad to interfere with the tendencies affecting this country, sterling will depreciate considerably during the next year or two. In reality, of course, it is impossible to assume that things will stand still abroad for any length of time. We have had to work on that assumption in this chapter so as to simplify the examination of factors having a direct bearing on sterling. We now propose to go a step further and examine in the next two chapters how sterling and gold are likely to be affected by developments in the United States and France.

CHAPTER IV

GOLD AND THE DOLLAR

AMONG the international factors that are likely to affect sterling the tendency of the dollar is by far the most important. A depreciation of the dollar is bound to be followed by a depreciation of sterling, not merely because it is the aim of the British authorities to prevent the sterling-dollar rate from departing permanently and substantially from its old parity, but also because an undervaluation of the dollar inevitably causes an adverse change in our trade balance. Great Britain cannot afford to allow the dollar to be undervalued against sterling. Experience throughout 1933–1934 showed that, in the long run, sterling follows the downward tendency of the dollar. It is most unlikely that the British Government would think of stabilising sterling until the definite level of the dollar had been ascertained. Meanwhile, President Roosevelt's policy dictates the pace at which sterling will depreciate.

Between April 1933 and February 1934 the depreciation of the dollar was the most important factor in influencing indirectly the London price of gold by causing sterling to depreciate. The direct influence of the gold policy adopted by President Roosevelt in October 1933 upon the sterling price of gold was negligible, for until January 31, 1934, when the price of gold was fixed at 35 dollars an ounce, the American gold price was hopelessly out of touch with the London gold price. The gradual raising of the official American buying price for gold between October 1933 and February 1934 affected the sterling price of gold through the intermediary of its effect upon the dollar exchange which, in turn, influenced sterling.

In January 1934 the dollar was provisionally stabilised, and its importance as an active factor in determining the sterling price of gold has declined. At the time of writing, the dollar factor is in the background. From time to time it makes itself felt, and it may reappear in full strength at any moment. Sooner or later President Roosevelt's monetary policy will become once again the most important influence in the London gold market. The nature and extent of this influence will depend upon the measures President Roosevelt chooses. Will he devalue the dollar once more, or will he inflate without devaluation? That is the question. That he will do one or the other is a foregone conclusion; he is commited to raising commodity prices, by fair means or foul, and it is now amply evident that there is no hope of a substantial rise in the price-level or a trade revival without adopting wholeheartedly either of the two alternatives. For the present, President Roosevelt hesitates and keeps on postponing decisive action. He hopes that by flirting both with inflation and with a sound financial policy he may be able to get the best of both worlds. Sooner or later he will have to realise the futility of such hopes and make up his mind one way or another. And, as he is an astute politician who knows on which side his bread is buttered, there can be no doubt that he will choose the course that secures for him the support of the West and Middle West.

If President Roosevelt embarks upon inflation without devaluation, the immediate result will probably be an appreciation of sterling, for prices in the United States will then tend to rise faster than in the United Kingdom. From this point of view, it will matter little whether inflation assumes the form of extensive subsidies to producers and consumers, or public works on a large scale, or the financing of a budgetary deficit through an increase of the note issue. Indeed, the mere anticipation of a new move in this policy would be sufficient to cause the dollar to depreciate in terms of sterling. The immediate effect would be a fall in the London price of gold. In the long run, however, a readjustment would take place; sterling would in all probability depreciate and return to the vicinity of its old parity, either through the deterioration of the British trade balance, or through the policy pursued by the Exchange Equalisation Account. It is an open secret that the Treasury regards the rate of 4·86 as the level round which the sterling dollar rate will have to settle. Any appreciation above that level could only produce a temporary effect upon the price of gold.

The second alternative is the devaluation of the dollar to 50 cents. President Roosevelt has obtained authority from Congress to go up to that limit, and the chances are that sooner or later he will make use of his powers. It is undoubtedly a much more effective way of raising prices than attempts at internal inflation. It is likely to meet with much less opposition on the part of the United States Treasury, which is anxious to avoid any action that interferes with its ability to borrow on reasonable terms. Indeed, there is so much to be said for it, and so very little against it, that most people regard the devaluation of the dollar to 50 cents as a mere question of time. Such a devaluation of the dollar would produce no direct and immediate effect on the London price of gold. The increase in the official American gold price from 35 dollars to 41·34 dollars an ounce would result in a corresponding depreciation of the dollar in terms of sterling and would not, therefore, affect automatically the sterling price of gold. As, however, sterling would in the long run follow the depreciation of the dollar, there would gradually be a corresponding rise in the sterling price of gold as and when the depreciation took place. A devaluation of the dollar to 50 cents would result in a depreciation of the dollar to ten shillings and this means a rise in the London market price of gold to 169s. 8d. This figure may be regarded as the minimum to which the London price of gold can reasonably be expected to rise.

It is possible, and even probable, that the devaluation of the dollar to 50 cents would not in itself be sufficient to produce the desired effect. A reduction of the gold value of the dollar by 9 cents would probably prove to be insufficient to bring back commodity prices to their 1926 level. An inflationist Congress would most probably demand a much more drastic devaluation. It remains to be seen how far President Roosevelt and the adherents of sound, or relatively sound, finance will be able to resist their pressure. Conceivably the dollar will be devalued in several stages to well below 50 cents. The question is whether sterling would follow it indefinitely. Anxious as the British Government is to maintain the sterling-dollar rate around its old parity, it is doubtful whether sterling would be made to follow the dollar beyond a certain stage. Should extreme inflationism gain control in the United States, in all probability the official British policy would be to await the adjustment of economic parities before adjusting sterling to the dollar. This means that, if the dollar is depreciated to, say, 20 cents and internal prices in the United States rise by 50 per cent, then it is sufficient for our purpose to depreciate sterling to a rate corresponding to a 35-cents dollar. There is at least a fair probability that the devaluation policy will be followed by a depreciation of sterling beneath ten shillings and a rise in the London price of gold above 169s. 8d.

The probable effect of the dollar factor upon the London price of gold may be summarised as follows: If there is inflation in the United States without a devaluation of the dollar, there will be a temporary appreciation of sterling and a temporary drop in the price of gold. In the longrun, however, both sterling and gold will tend to return to their old level. If the dollar is devalued to 50 cents, sterling will gradually depreciate to ten shillings and gold will likewise rise to 169s. 8d. If the dollar is devalued to below 50 cents, sterling may, or may not, follow it and gold may, or may not, rise beyond 169s. 8d. Thus the dollar factor will in no case cause a fall in the price of gold except, perhaps, temporarily; the chances are that it will cause quite a substantial rise in the price of the metal.

There remains one factor to be considered in this connection, namely, the policy of the American Exchange Equalisation Account. Official American purchases of gold, silver, or sterling may cause the dollar to depreciate against sterling. Up to now such operations have been conducted on a comparatively modest scale, and have not led to a depreciation of the dollar in terms of sterling. In fact, they have not even prevented the gradual depreciation of sterling in terms of dollars during March-October 1934. As far as it is possible to ascertain, the object of official American intervention in the international market has been to counteract the effect upon the dollar of the favourable trade balance of the United States. It is probable that intervention will continue to be confined to these limits in future, in which case the operations of the American Exchange Equalisation Account will not cause even a temporary fall in the London price of gold, though they may prevent a rise in the price which would otherwise take place.

It would not be wise, however, to rule out the possibility of a more active and aggressive intervention on the part of the American authorities. President Roosevelt's attitude has been and will be the most incalculable of all factors. He changes his policies and tactics with the rapidity of a quick-change artiste, and the world has to be prepared for surprises from that quarter. The last surprise he sprang on an unsuspecting world was the announcement of his silver-buying policy. This was over three months ago, so that a new surprise is overdue. Conceivably it may assume the nature of intensive intervention in the form of buying sterling or gold or silver. Should the sterling dollar rate decline below 4·86 it is almost certain that such action would be taken from Washington. The activities of the American Exchange Equalisation Account will have to be considered, therefore, as a potential bear point for gold.

The British authorities, it is hardly necessary to add, would not remain inactive in the above eventuality. They would certainly take up the challenge and would endeavour to counteract the action of the American Exchange Equalisation Account to cause an appreciation of sterling. So long as the American authorities are prepared to sell gold at a fixed price while the British authorities are not, the former will be at a grave disadvantage in a currency contest. The British Exchange Equalisation Account need not necessarily take the risk of buying dollars in order to keep sterling down; it could achieve the same object by buying francs and withdrawing gold from the Bank of France. The result would be an appreciation of the franc in terms of dollars and the flow of gold from the United States to France, which again would readjust the dollar to its old level. The American authorities are probably aware that, as things are, they would get the worse of a currency war, and this is probably one of the reasons why they do not attempt aggressive action. The probability of a fall in the London price of gold through such action is, therefore, very small.

To sum up: although the dollar factor may, taking a short view, cause either a rise or a fall in the sterling price of gold, it must eventually prove a bull point for the metal.

CHAPTER V

GOLD AND THE FRANC

We have seen in the last two chapters that the factors affecting sterling, either directly or through their influence upon the dollar, will tend to cause a further rise in the London price of gold in the long-run. We now propose to examine the probable influence of the tendencies of the French franc. Between April and October 1934 the firmness of the franc was largely responsible for the rise in the price of gold in London. The return of confidence in the franc resulted in the wholesale repatriation of the French funds which took refuge in London during the crisis of 1933–1934. Other Continental balances followed suit, and at the same time British funds were attracted to Paris by the higher rates of interest prevailing there. The result has been a low but persistent depreciation of sterling throughout the summer, which in its turn has caused a corresponding rise in the price of gold. It is true that, at the same time, the premium of gold over the price based on the franc rate has declined, owing to the slackening of demand for gold for hoarding purposes. While, however, the decline of the premium on account of this factor was barely sixpence, the increase in the basic rate on account of the appreciation of francs was something like five shillings. This indicates the relative importance of the factor of exchange rate and that of market supply and demand.

The question arises as to whether the appreciation of

francs in terms of sterling, caused by the return of confidence in the franc, will be of lasting nature. At the time of writing it is widely believed in France that the French crisis is a matter of the past, and that it will not recur. Intelligent opinion abroad, however, is sceptical about this. Some doubt exists as to whether the efforts to balance the budget will prove successful, especially if, as is probable, the international political situation necessitates an increase in armament expenditure. The position of the French Treasury is none too strong, and a deterioration in the budgetary situation, coupled with a return of the wave of distrust among the investing public, might easily bring about a crisis of the Treasury, such as threatened to cause inflation at the end of 1933 and the beginning of 1934.

As the author explained in detail in his book *France's Crisis*, the financial, economic, psychological, moral, and political factors all work against the franc. He is convinced that eventually France will have to decide to devalue the franc. For the time being, however, the French Government is determined to maintain the franc at its present level. Even if the crisis were to return, the technical position of the Bank of France is strong enough to resist the adverse pressure for a long time.

Meanwhile, renewed troubles in France would result in an appreciation of sterling. Political troubles, and a deterioration in the economic and financial situation, would bring about a flight to the pound such as we have seen repeatedly during the last three years. The rise in sterling would then cause a fall in the price of gold. There would probably be witnessed a revival of French demand for gold for hoarding purposes, which would increase the premium, but this increase would be offset several times over by the decline of the basic price on account of the appreciation of sterling. It remains to be seen what attitude the Exchange Equalisation Account would take up towards the unwanted rise in sterling. In all probability it would oppose the trend by buying francs and withdrawing gold from the Bank of France.

Apart from its desire to prevent an appreciation of sterling, the Exchange Equalisation Account is also anxious to replenish its gold reserves which have been depleted to a large extent through the pressure on sterling during 1934. The Exchange Equalisation Account would, therefore, probably operate on a large scale in the foreign exchange market to counteract the buying pressure on sterling. It would not be reasonable, however, to assume that its operations would altogether prevent a rise in sterling. Judging by official statements as well as past experience, it is not the policy of the Exchange Equalisation Account to peg sterling rigidly against a rising trend. It usually aims at moderating, regulating, and delaying the movement, instead of stopping it altogether. There is no reason to suppose that it will be otherwise on the next occasion.

Taking a short view, the franc factor will most probably be the cause of a fall in the London price of gold. It is impossible to foresee how far this tendency will go and when it will end. If France's troubles blow over once more—for the time being at any rate—the French funds seeking refuge in London will be again repatriated and sterling will relapse. Gold will then tend to recover to its old level. Indeed, judging by past experience, the chances are that, by the time the French funds are repatriated, the sterling-franc rate will be lower, and the London price of gold will be higher, than it was before the beginning of the flight to the pound. For, as we pointed out in Chapter III., it is the practice of the Exchange Equalisation Account to retain part of the gold acquired through the flight to the pound. It will not intervene to the same extent to prevent a fall of sterling as it did in order to prevent a rise. Moreover, the recovery of sterling, however temporary, will produce an adverse effect upon the British trade balance, and this factor will also accentuate the relapse.

It is possible that, under the inexorable pressure of developments, the French Government will decide some time in 1935 to devalue the franc. This would not in itself affect the London price of gold any more than would another devaluation of the dollar. The franc would depreciate in terms of sterling to the extent of the reduction of its gold content, and there is no reason why this change should affect automatically the London price of gold. It may, however, produce an indirect and gradual effect upon the gold price if, in consequence of a devaluation of the franc, the British trade balance were to deteriorate. In that case sterling might further depreciate, and the sterling price of gold might rise. Thus, taking a long view, the devaluation of the franc is likely to cause a rise in the London price of gold, and not, as is popularly believed, a fall.

Possibly, instead of devaluing the franc, the French Government might suspend the gold standard and allow the franc to depreciate. Such a solution would be even more unpopular in France than devaluation. It is nevertheless possible that the Government would have to resort to it owing to the delay in passing legislation for altering the gold contents of the franc. Should France suspend the gold standard it is certain that all other countries of the Gold Group would immediately follow her example. An entirely new situation would then arise. How, in the changed circumstances, would the price of gold behave? This question is causing more worry to many holders of gold and gold-mining shares than almost any other, for the view is held that, in the chaos that would follow the suspension of the gold standard by France, almost anything might happen.

Doubtless, the suspension of the gold standard in France would complicate matters for a while. But it is none the less possible to form an opinion about the probable effect of the development upon the price of gold. The most important question is, whether or not the United States would also suspend the provisional and limited gold standard established in February 1934. If the American monetary authorities continue to buy and sell gold for international purposes at a fixed price, then there is no reason why the suspension of the gold standard by France should affect the London market price of gold, which will henceforth depend entirely on the sterling-dollar rate. Even if the sterling-franc rate should rise to 100, it would not cause a fall in the London price of gold so long as the American gold price of 35 dollars per ounce remained effective, and so long as the sterling-dollar rate remained practically unchanged. We must consider, however, how the sterling-dollar rate would be affected by the suspension of the gold standard by France. There would be a wholesale flight from the franc and from the other Continental currencies. It remains to be seen whether the majority of Continental capital would seek refuge in London or in New

York. This largely depends upon conditions prevailing in Wall Street and in the United States in general at the time of the suspension of the gold standard by France. It seems probable that, unless there happened to be a boom in Wall Street, the bulk of the Continental capital would play for safety and come to London. As a result, sterling would tend to appreciate in terms of dollars. The Exchange Equalisation Account would, however, be in a position to counteract this tendency by purchases of dollars and of gold. In any case, once the first shock of the flight from the Continental currencies is over, sterling would tend to readjust itself to its old level as a result of the adverse effect of the depreciation of those currencies upon the British trade balance. Thus, even in the absence of any effective action on the part of the Exchange Equalisation Account, the chances are that any fall in the London price of gold caused by the appreciation of sterling would be of but temporary duration. Indeed, if the Continental currencies were to go too far in their depreciation, the United States authorities would probably decide to make a further cut in the gold value of the dollar, in which case the British authorities would allow sterling to move in sympathy. Thus in the long run the depreciation of Continental currencies would probably cause a further rise in the London price of gold.

If, following upon the suspension of the gold standard in France, the United States also suspends the provisional and limited gold standard that has operated since February 1934, then none of the exchange rates will have any direct influence upon the London price of gold. In such conditions, the price will be governed entirely by market supply and demand.

There is a high degree of probability, amounting almost to certainty, that in such circumstances, the price of gold would undergo a spectacular rise, since the suspension of the gold standard by all countries would limit the supply of gold to the amount available in the market. None of the Central Banks would be prepared any longer to sell gold on demand. On the other hand, Central Banks and Governments would continue to be keen buyers of gold. The Exchange Equalisation Account would do its utmost to secure the largest possible amount of gold, because that would be the only means at its disposal for counteracting a rising tendency of sterling. Amidst the currency chaos the authorities would not dare to risk holding francs or dollars, so that the only alternative to influencing sterling through gold purchases would be to leave it to its fate. The monetary authorities of other countries, especially of the United States, would also become keen bidders for gold for the same reason. There would also be an increase in private hoarding of gold. As a result of the growing uncertainty caused by the suspension of the gold standard throughout the world, the number of people anxious to buy gold would increase considerably. It is probable that their competition, in addition to that of the monetary authorities, would raise the London price of gold to a fantastic level. Possibly this exaggerated rise would be purely temporary, and, on the advent of stabilisation, the official price of gold would be fixed well under the high record. At the same time, the currency depreciation race that would probably take place if all countries came off gold would go a long way towards consolidating the price at the level to which reckless competition had raised gold.

Neither a devaluation nor a depreciation of the franc is likely to occur in the near future. In all probability the franc will be defended, for some time at any rate, against any adverse tendencies. There will, however, be a flight to the pound, similar to that of 1933–1934, which will cause a temporary appreciation of sterling and a temporary fall in the London price of gold. Taking a short view, therefore, the price of gold is likely to fall rather than rise, unless the dollar is devalued before the flight to the pound occurs. Should that be the case, the falling tendency caused by the flight from the franc and the rising tendency caused by the devaluation of the dollar may possibly more or less cancel each other out in the short-run. In the long-run, however, sterling will follow the dollar, and gold will then recover its temporary loss. While speculators, who have acquired gold or gold-mining shares for the sake of making a profit on an early rise, have good reason to be concerned about the immediate prospects, investors for whom it is only the long view that matters have no reason to worry. Even though gold may fall within, say, the next six months from the time of writing, it is certain to rise to high levels within the next year or two.

CHAPTER VI

GOLD HOARDING

It has become the fashion, during the last decade or two, to denounce gold as a "barbarous relic" and an "old-fashioned fetish". Economists and practical bankers of distinction have declared the monetary system of gold to be "unscientific", ridiculing the stubbornness with which the world clings to gold. They have prophesied that in a more enlightened age the gold stocks accumulated by nations will be worth no more than scrap iron. Nothing they have said, however, has so far produced the least effect upon the instinct of the public to seek refuge in gold hoarding during times of crisis. However logical and convincing the arguments of the opponents of the gold standard may be, instinct is stronger than their teachings.

Before the crisis it appeared as if the "scientific" monetary conception had been making progress towards defeating the prejudice of the public in favour of gold. Since the war practically every country has abandoned the pre-war practice of issuing gold coins, and most of the pre-war coins have been withdrawn from circulation. The gold bullion standard and the gold exchange standard have taken the place of the former gold standard. It was, indeed, believed that the public had lost its desire for hoarding gold. The experience of the crisis has proved that this change was entirely on the surface. So long as all went more or less smoothly, the public did not feel any need for hoarding. The moment, however, that things began to go wrong, the gold hoarding instinct came to the fore in almost every country.

In Central Europe, where post-war inflation was at its worst, it was only natural that the public should play for safety. Those who could afford to do so transferred their wealth to London, Holland or Switzerland and converted it into gold deposits. In France, despite the strong technical position of the franc, a hoarding fever seized the population from 1931 onwards. By means of withdrawals from the Bank of France or purchases from abroad, gold to the value of many milliards of francs has been hoarded. Within a few months of the beginning of the crisis, there was no more accommodation left in the safes of banks, notwithstanding the fact that the greater part of large hoards were transferred abroad, and that the greater part of small hoards were kept in the proverbial stockings. In the United States, the hoarding fever began to assume spectacular dimensions during the months that preceded the suspension of the gold standard in 1933. Although, after the suspension of the gold standard, the authorities organised systematic drives to retrieve the gold withdrawn for internal hoarding, a large part of the amount withdrawn has remained hidden.

There are two countries, Great Britain and India, whose attitude towards gold hoarding during the crisis has been in sharp contrast to that of the rest of the world. While all the other nations were busily engaged in hoarding, both the British and Indian populations were dishoarding their gold stocks. In the case of Great Britain the amount so released was comparatively moderate, but the volume of Indian gold thrown on the world market constituted a most important factor.

According to one explanation the British attitude is the result of the superiority of the "financial civilisation" of the British nation, a superiority which manifests itself in the extensive use of cheques, in the almost complete absence of hoarding, and in the sensible attitude of depositors in times of crisis, etc. Hoarding is considered a sign of inferiority, and it is regarded as a matter of *noblesse oblige* for the British people to keep aloof from it. Flattering as this explanation may be, it cannot be accepted without addition and qualification. Unquestionably, the absence of any desire to hoard, and the gesture of dishoarding when everybody else was hoarding, was due in part to the superior "financial civilisation" and to the exceptionally steady nerves of the British public. In part, however, it was also due to the absence of any inflationary experience, such as the public in most Continental countries had undergone during and after the war. British people do not know what it means to witness the depreciation of their currency overnight; to see the value of their savings dwindle through currency depreciation to a fraction of its original amount; to watch the prices marked in shop windows changed every few minutes and to see the price of meals in restaurants raised while they are having them. Had they undergone such experiences, steel nerves and superior financial culture would not have deterred them from hoarding during the crisis.

Another reason why British people were dishoarding instead of hoarding in 1931–1932 lies in the characteristic British habit of not knowing when they are defeated. It is a popular story on the Continent that

Wellington won the battle of Waterloo simply because he did not know that, according to all recognised rules of strategy, he was defeated and ought to have run away in consequence. Similarly, sterling retained its intrinsic value throughout the crisis because the British people did not know that, according to all rules of monetary science, the pound was to depreciate internally after the suspension of the gold standard. They firmly believed all along that "a pound is a pound" as far as they were concerned, no matter what the exchange rates were. When bullion dealers and jewellers offered them 27s. 6d. for a sovereign they were only too keen to take what they considered to be their profit—hence the dishoarding of sovereigns by the million.

The wholesale dishoarding of gold in India was partly the result of the long depression which compelled the population to fall back upon their last reserve represented by their gold hoards. At the same time, confidence in the pound must also have played an important part in provoking the movement of dishoarding. The rupee was stabilised in relation to the pound, and the Indian public trusted to the British administration to prevent it depreciating internally. The prices obtained for gold were tempting and the Indian population, which before the crisis was hoarding on a gigantic scale, began to dishoard while almost all other nations were hoarding.

Much has been said and written about the moral aspects of gold hoarding. It is sometimes denounced as "unpatriotic" in the same way as the flight from the national currency is unpatriotic. Hoarders of gold are sometimes compared with "rats that leave the sinking ship". It is doubtless convenient to discourage hoarding by exaggerating its moral aspects. In reality there seems to be nothing derogatory in making use of the right offered by law to the holders of banknotes to withdraw gold from the Central Banks. So long as this right exists, there is no reason for moral indignation against those who make use of it. If their action is inconvenient, the authorities have the remedy in their hands. It is sheer hypocrisy to maintain nominally the convertibility of notes and to use in practice most drastic methods of "dissuading" anyone who wants to exercise his right. This was done in Great Britain during the war and also to some extent in France during the crisis. The United States Government went even further. While the Federal Reserve banks were prepared to pay out gold until the suspension of the gold standard in March 1933, subsequently legislation was passed compelling those who had withdrawn gold to surrender it to the authorities. Such measures amount to confiscatory legislation.

The experience of hoarders of gold in the United States has led to the conclusion that London is practically the only safe place for hoarding gold. Notwithstanding all the nonsense that is being written on the subject, it is legitimate for foreigners residing abroad to hoard gold in the United Kingdom to an unlimited amount. This was made plain in the text of the Currency and Bank Notes Act of 1928, and also in the statement made in the House of Commons by the Government spokesman in the course of the debate. In practice the privileged position of foreigners was made plain in 1931, when exchange restrictions were introduced in this country. While British residents were forbidden to export their capital abroad in the form of gold, there was nothing to prevent foreign holders from withdrawing their gold deposits from London.

In law, the limit of British hoarding of gold is fixed at £10,000 per person, above which amount the Bank of England is entitled to call in the gold and pay for it at the statutory buying price of 84s. 10d. per ounce. The limit of £10,000 is very liberal, and a large family or a firm with a number of partners or directors, each of whom is entitled to hoard £10,000, could safely hoard quite substantial amounts. In any case, there is no likelihood of the application of the law against private hoarders. Its object was merely to prevent bankers from accumulating gold reserves of their own. At the time of the passing of the Act, Mr. McKenna was suspected, rightly or wrongly, of harbouring such intentions, which the Bank of England was anxious to forestall. The only time the clause was applied was immediately after the suspension of the gold standard, when the Bank of England broke the hearts of some of the Scottish banks by compelling them to surrender their gold stocks at par. Apart from this, the clause has lain dormant and, unless conditions change radically, it is not likely to be applied. Indeed, the Government has actually recognised officially that British hoarders of gold are entitled to sell their holdings at a premium. In a statement made by the Chancellor of the Exchequer in 1931, British hoarders of sovereigns were, in fact, urged to sell their coins at a premium. Taking into consideration the liberal attitude of the authorities towards British holders of gold, and the traditional discrimination in matters of money in favour of foreigners, it may be safely assumed that foreign holders of gold in London have nothing to fear in the form of action on the part of the Government.

It is difficult indeed to understand the motive of the violent opposition displayed in some quarters to the hoarding of foreign gold in London. If the gold were withdrawn from the Bank of England there might be some justification for disapproval. It is, in reality, either imported from abroad or bought in the open market in London. If the gold is imported from abroad it cannot possibly have any influence on sterling, while, if it is bought in the London market, then it tends to strengthen sterling in so far as the buyers have to buy sterling with which to pay for the gold. The unsettling influence of the foreign gold deposits in London, estimated at around £150 millions, is not nearly as strong as that of an equivalent amount of foreign sterling balances. While the withdrawal of balances might cause inconvenient exchange fluctuations, the withdrawal of gold deposits is not likely to disturb the exchange. This question, with all its technical details, is discussed at some length in Appendix II.

While it is difficult to see the objections to foreign gold deposits, their advantages from a British point of view are obvious. These deposits constitute sources of profit for London banks, safe deposit companies, bullion brokers, insurance companies, etc. At a time when banking activity in general is none too profitable, the commissions earned in connection with the purchase and sale of foreign gold, and the charges on deposits kept in the vaults, constitute a welcome item. Many of the gold deposits change hands frequently and this increases considerably the turnover of the London bullion market.

From a broader point of view the presence of large foreign gold deposits in London can only be beneficial. In Chapter V. we described a situation which might possibly arise if all countries were to suspend the gold standard. We pointed out that, in such circumstances, the only way in which the Exchange Equalisation Account could counteract an unwanted appreciation of sterling would be through gold purchases, and the larger the amounts it could purchase, the more effective its policy would be. If, thanks to the presence of large foreign gold deposits, the turnover in the London gold market were high, this would assist the efforts of the authorities to no slight degree. Looking further ahead, the existence of foreign gold deposits in London will facilitate the task of the Bank of England in increasing its gold reserve after the stabilisation of sterling. With the return of confidence, holders will gradually sell their gold. It depends, of course, upon the exchange rates whether it will be more profitable for them to sell it to the Bank of England or to some other Central Bank; but, owing to the fact that holders would have to pay the cost of transport and insurance if they were to send their gold abroad, the Bank of England stands a good chance of securing the bulk of the hoards. Their presence in London amounts in practice to a free option in favour of the Bank.

It may be objected that a heavy increase in the Bank's gold reserve might lead to gold inflation. This question is dealt with in detail in later chapters. Here it is sufficient to point out that, strangely enough, the quarters from which opposition to foreign gold hoardings originate are themselves inflationist. They do not appear to realise that in attacking foreign gold hoardings they are in reality supporting their opponents, the orthodox deflationists. It is true that what they suggest is that the Government should confiscate the foreign gold in London and should pay for it at the statutory buying price. As, however, such action is legally impossible—it would amount to confiscation—the only result their anti-hoarding campaign can possibly produce is to frighten hoarders into transferring their gold to some other centre, which means that the ultimate chances of the Bank of England acquiring the gold are reduced. Thus, in effect, the anti-gold crusade of the Beaverbrook Press is inconsistent with the attitude of that group towards monetary policy in general. There is a still more glaring inconsistency between the anti-gold campaign and the Empire crusade of the Beaverbrook Press. About this more will be said in Chapter VIII.

It is, indeed, amazing to what lengths the anti-gold campaign of the Beaverbrook Press is prepared to go. It began with the comic episode of the City Editor of the *Evening Standard* buying a gold bar in an effort to prove that holders of gold were likely to suffer losses. Ever since then the price of gold has been rising almost incessantly, and Mr. Wade was compelled to sell his bar at a profit—much to his dismay. Most holders paid no heed to the warnings of their imminent doom, repeated to boredom by the Beaverbrook papers. Thereupon, the *Daily Express* called upon the Government to take steps in the matter. So long as this campaign confined itself to demanding new legislation enabling the Government to seize the foreign gold deposits, no exception could be taken to it. The crusaders, however, went a good deal further. They published misleading statements about the existing legislation, by maintaining that, under the Currency and Bank Notes Act of 1928, the Government is entitled to seize foreign hoards. When the blunder was pointed out, they took refuge behind a screen of sophistries, arguing that the law exempts "foreign holdings" but not "foreign hoards". In reality the legal aspects of the question are unequivocal, which fact the reader can ascertain for himself in Appendix V, which contains the relevant official texts. While the wisdom or unwisdom of changing the existing legislation is a matter of opinion, the absence of any right to call in foreign gold on the basis of the existing legislation is a matter of fact. Indeed, it is extremely unlikely that legislative steps would be taken on the lines suggested by Lord Beaverbrook. In responsible quarters the advantages of encouraging rather than discouraging foreign gold deposits in London is doubtless duly realised. In any case, not even Lord Beaverbrook's threats of a revolution in the event of his demand being disregarded, would induce the Government to pass legislation of a confiscatory nature. Somehow it is difficult to visualise an enraged British crowd, similar to that of Paris on February 6, 1934, breaking through the police cordon in order to sweep away the Government which refuses to confiscate foreign property!

The Government's attitude in the matter of gold and gold hoards was, in fact, defined at the Economic Conference, when at the meeting of one of the subcommittees the United States delegates proposed that a resolution be adopted affirming the right of Governments to call in hoarded gold at par. The proposal was rejected, as it met with the determined opposition of both British and French delegates.

From the point of view of the effect of the antihoarding campaign upon the London price of gold, it is essential to make it clear that any fluctuations in hoarding only affect the premium of gold on the gold exchanges. So long as there is one currency on a gold basis, wide movements in the premium will produce their correctives by bringing about withdrawals from Central Banks on a gold basis, or sales of gold to them, according to the case. Thus, even if the anti-gold group were to succeed in frightening a large number of people into selling their gold stocks in a hurry, it would merely affect the premium of gold so that the fall in the London price would be a fraction of 1 per cent. In reality there is no need to anticipate any such panicky liquidation of gold stocks. Although the anti-gold campaign results from time to time in a flood of enquiries by Continental holders as to whether there is any likelihood of confiscatory legislation being adopted, few, if any of them, have taken the threat sufficiently seriously to sell their hoardings on that account. Having disregarded Lord Beaverbrook's threats a hundred times, they are not likely to become frightened on the hundred and first occasion. To all intents and purposes the anti-gold crusade has failed.

In all other respects, the causes which induced people to hoard gold still exist. Conditions are still uncertain, and conservative investors still prefer to play for safety. They are still prepared to lose interest rather than take risks, especially as, owing to the low yield rates on good-class investments, the loss is none too big. So long as money is cheap the temptation to liquidate gold stocks and re-invest the proceeds in conservative securities is none too strong. World conditions would have to go a long way towards consolidation before the present low interest rates would be sufficient inducement for most holders to liquidate their stocks.

CHAPTER VII

THE RATE OF STABILISATION

In the foregoing chapters we have been dealing with influences upon the price of gold which are likely to be at work prior to the stabilisation of sterling. The next step is to come to a conclusion as to the level at which sterling is likely to be stabilised. Admittedly, in many quarters it is doubted whether sterling will ever be stabilised at all in relation to gold. We propose to deal with this question in the next chapter. In the meantime we shall try to weigh the probabilities as to the level of its stabilisation—if and when it is stabilised.

It is characteristic of the conflict of opinion that exists regarding practically every question relating to gold that, while one school is convinced that sterling will never be linked to gold again, another school is equally convinced that stabilisation is imminent. Whenever sterling remains comparatively stable for even a few weeks only, rumours of impending stabilisation come into circulation, only to be dispelled by the next violent movement that follows the brief period of stability. In the autumn of 1934, when sterling was weak owing to the seasonal factor and the dollar rate was approaching its old parity of 4·86, it was widely believed that the sterling-dollar rate was deliberately being brought back to its old parity in order to stabilise it there.

In reality, an early stabilisation of sterling seems

most unlikely. Having learnt their lesson through the mistake made in 1925, the British authorities will probably be very careful to make sure that when they stabilise sterling again they will stand a good chance of being able to maintain it at its new level without undue sacrifices. It is most unlikely that sterling will be stabilised before President Roosevelt has made up his mind what to do with the dollar. Notwithstanding a recent broadcast statement of the President, in which he was inclined to "flirt" with orthodox monetary principles, the day when he will make up his mind to stabilise the dollar definitely is still very remote. Nor is the British Government likely to stabilise until it is reasonably certain that the Gold Group will maintain its present parities. At present, conditions in France and elsewhere are still too obscure to make it advisable to assume that they would be able and willing to retain their currencies at par in any circumstances.

Another question which is likely to delay the British decision is that of war debts. Although payment of war debts is suspended, the British Government has every intention of coming to terms with the United States Government, provided that Washington is prepared to be reasonable. It might take years before Administration and Congress get into a reasonable frame of mind; and in the meantime there can be no question of stabilisation. Apart from all this, considerations of internal policy are also against an early return to gold. Rightly or wrongly, the gold standard has become extremely unpopular in this country. The public has come to regard it as a root of all evil, especially as since the suspension of the gold standard conditions in this country have improved materially.

It would be, therefore, a most unpopular act to return to gold. The National Government could hardly afford to do so before the next General Election. To stabilise now would drive millions of electors into the Socialist camp.

It seems probable, therefore, that it will take at least a year or two before the Government thinks of stabilising. Meanwhile, as we have seen in Chapters III., IV., and V., the factors that affect sterling, dollar, and franc are likely to cause in the long run a further rise in the London price of gold. We have seen that the possible devaluation of the dollar and of the gold currencies would work in that direction; that the necessity for this country to increase its gold stock will tend to raise the price of gold; that in the case of the suspension of the gold standard by all countries a depreciation race and a demand for hoarding purposes might raise the price of gold to a fantastic level. All these are temporary influences. They need not necessarily determine the choice of the definite level at which sterling will be stabilised, but to a large extent they are likely to influence the Government's decision. If temporary influences were to raise the price of gold up to, say, 340s. per ounce, it would not necessarily mean that the Government would have to stabilise sterling at the level of about 5s., but the rate of stabilisation would certainly be higher than it would be had the price remained at its present level, or if it were to rise to 200s. only. If temporary influences cause sterling to depreciate and to remain at its low level for some length of time, then stabilisation at a higher level would involve deflation. If there is one thing which is certain amidst all the monetary uncertainties, it is that in no circumstances will the British Government embark upon a deflationary monetary policy. The time when it was possible to decide upon such a policy behind closed doors is past; the public in this country knows too much by now about its consequences to put up with it.

Thus, it is reasonable to assume that, while the price of gold is not likely to be stabilised at the peak of its rise, its definite figure will be fixed sufficiently high to avoid the necessity of deflation. What that level will be, no one can foretell; but, as we pointed out in an earlier chapter, the price of 169s. 8d. per ounce, being the equivalent to the ten shilling-pound, can safely be considered the minimum.

It stands to reason that a final decision about the rate of stabilisation of sterling will not be reached without regard to the rates of stabilisation chosen by other Governments. An attempt will doubtless be made to come to an international agreement about the various new parities. The negotiations conducted for that purpose will be extremely difficult. Most Governments will want to avoid at all costs having an overvalued currency. As it is bordering on the impossible to ascertain the economic parities, they will want to be on the safe side by undervaluing their currencies. It is, obviously, arithmetically impossible for all currencies to be undervalued in relation to each other. The chances are that the Governments which are the most anxious to stabilise will be inclined, to some degree, to agree to a moderate overvaluation of their currencies in terms of those of Governments which are the least anxious to stabilise. There will undoubtedly be endless haggling about the rates of stabilisation, and a deadlock might easily be reached.

In some quarters, indeed, it is feared that no agreement will be possible, and that for this reason the world will be unlikely to return to the gold standard. The author is not nearly so pessimistic on this point. Difficult as it will be to come to an agreement, sooner or later an understanding will be reached which, if not equally satisfactory to everybody, will not at any rate create untenable positions. We said above that it is impossible for all currencies to be undervalued in relation to each other. It is, however, quite possible for all currencies to be undervalued in terms of gold. This is exactly what is likely to happen. The overvaluation of a currency places the country concerned at a disadvantage if it necessitates direct deflation to adjust its prices to the world level. If, however, all currencies are undervalued in terms of gold, then there can be no question of any deflation in any country. A rise in commodity prices is likely to follow everywhere. The difference between the national price-levels created through the undervaluation of some currencies and the overvaluation of others can be offset by the different degree in which prices are allowed to rise in various countries.

It is on such a basis that an international agreement on the new gold parities is conceivable. Failing that, every country would choose its own level of stabilisation without regard to the others, and the chances are that countries with overvalued currencies would in the long run have to devalue once more. The final result would thus be more or less the same as if they had all agreed in the first instance upon undervaluation of their currencies against gold. The difference is that the result could be achieved much more smoothly through international agreement. Thus, whether stabilisation is achieved through agreement or in the absence of agreement, the chances are that the price of gold will eventually be stabilised at a fairly high level.

An important reason why most Governments would prefer stabilising the price of gold at a high level is that it would increase the margin of their gold stocks for indispensable and immediate requirements. It is true that if commodity prices rise to a corresponding degree the margin thus created would disappear. However, as the author will try to show in a later chapter, commodity prices are not likely to adjust themselves in full to the changed parities and whatever rise there is likely to be will take time. The decline in the margin of gold reserves through a rise in prices will be slow and will not be complete. This will be of great advantage to all countries because, during the earlier period while confidence is not altogether restored, they will possess a comfortable safety margin of gold reserve. There are many other reasons why the authorities of all countries will want ample gold reserves, as we shall see in later chapters.

Apart from the monetary considerations which will make it desirable for Central Banks to have ample safety margins, and to that end, to fix the definite price of gold at a high figure, there are also other considerations of great importance working in the same direction. It is generally admitted that excessive indebtedness since the war has been one of the major causes of the world economic crisis. The choice of a low rate of stabilisation—that is, a high gold price—would reduce considerably both internal and international indebtedness. While private indebtedness in Great Britain cannot be said to be excessive, the burden of the public debt is abnormal. A radical devaluation of the pound would greatly remedy this evil, as it would cause a rise in commodity prices which in turn would increase the yield of taxation, so that the relative burden of public debt would decline. In the United States, private indebtedness has assumed unbearable proportions while the public debt is also becoming increasingly heavy. There can be no return of lasting prosperity until this burden is reduced. In France, the result of deflation has been an increase of the burden of public debt to the limit of the nation's capacity. Both she and Italy would benefit immensely from a reduction of that burden by a devaluation of their currencies. The same may be said more or less to hold good for practically every country, since excessive public debt is a common evil throughout the civilised world.

The reduction of the real burden of public debt would go a long way towards easing the budgetary position of all countries. It would facilitate the Government's task of finding the necessary money for the inevitable increase of current and capital expenditure. Such increase is bound to take place in the first instance in connection with the rearmament race which is, unfortunately, inevitable. In the course of the next few years every Government will endeavour to spend more on national defence. This factor in itself is strong enough to compel Governments to choose a low rate of stabilisation for their currencies, so as to be able to provide for the budgetary requirements of national defence. If the alternative to drastic devaluation is the jeopardising of the nations' security, then few Governments are likely to hesitate to sacrifice orthodox monetary principles.

Another reason why there is every likelihood that

the eventual choice of a rate of stabilisation will be at low figures is the present demand in every country for public works of various kinds. To some extent, this demand is due to the desire to end the economic depression. But a much more important and more lasting influence in the same direction is the growing discontent among the working classes with existing housing conditions. Pressure of public opinion will compel Governments to embark upon ambitious housing schemes. Heavy expenditure for that purpose will contribute to the increase of the necessity for a drastic devaluation of currencies. While we were on the gold standard, such expenditure was resisted to the utmost for fear that it might drive this country off the gold standard. Being now off the gold standard this bogey no longer exists. The only "danger" is that expenditure running into hundreds of millions of pounds for slum clearance might necessitate the devaluation of the pound to, say, 8s. instead of 10s. Most people would consider such a risk well worth taking, in order to solve the housing problem.

The position, in this respect, is more or less identical in every country. Most currencies are already in the melting-pot, and those not yet there will be, sooner or later. That being the case, Governments will be inclined to adopt a less rigid attitude towards social capital expenditure than they have done in the past. All this is working towards the lowering of the level at which currencies will eventually be stabilised, which means that the ultimate price of gold will be higher.

Another factor which increases the probability of the choice of a high gold price is the possibility of a Socialist victory at the next General Election. We said above that the National Government is not likely to drive millions of electors into the Socialist camp by stabilising the pound before the General Election. If the General Election results in the advent of a Socialist Government, then the decision to fix the definite value of the pound will rest with that Government. Socialists are not likely to be influenced by those considerations of monetary orthodoxy that would deter a Conservative Government from deciding upon a really drastic devaluation. In any case, the pound would depreciate considerably through the return of a Socialist Government, partly because of the flight of capital and partly because of the increase in public expenditure that would take place under a Socialist régime. In such circumstances the decision of the Government to stabilise sterling at a very low level would merely confirm an existing state of affairs.

Monetary considerations alone would be sufficient to induce Governments to choose a low level for the stabilisation of their currencies. The need for very wide safety margins of gold reserves after the return to the gold standard is imperative. The changes in the economic structure of most countries during the crisis and the unsettled state of international trade will result in very wide fluctuations in trade balances. Nor is there any reason to hope that after the stabilisation of currencies such fluctuations would be gradually reduced to normal levels. The difference between working conditions in various countries, the different degree of application of inventions and methods of planning, and various other factors, will all work towards producing frequent surprise changes in international trade conditions. It is to the interest of all countries, if they want to maintain the stability of their currencies, to safeguard themselves against such surprises by possessing ample safety margins of gold reserves. The lower they stabilise their currencies, the wider will be their safety margins, and the stronger will be their chance of maintaining their currencies at the new level.

CHAPTER VIII

IS THE GOLD STANDARD DOOMED?

In the preceding chapter we assumed throughout that the world in general and Great Britain in particular will eventually return to the gold standard, and that the only question of importance from the point of view of the price of gold is the rate that will be chosen for the stabilisation of currencies. This assumption is not accepted by everyone. Many people doubt whether we shall ever return to the gold standard; they believe that sooner or later the whole world will abandon the system. This question is of the utmost importance from the viewpoint of the future price of gold. For, if the gold standard is abandoned and the huge monetary stocks of gold are thrown on the market, a slump in the price of gold must follow. Of course, it is gross exaggeration to maintain that, even in such conditions, "the value of gold would be reduced to that of scrap iron", as radical economists often prophesy. The demand for gold for industrial, scientific, and other purposes is not sufficient in itself to maintain the metal at a relatively high value. On the other hand, hoarding would not cease with the decision of the monetary authorities to discard gold. Nevertheless, it is beyond doubt that the demonetisation of gold would reduce its price to a fraction of its present figure. For this reason, the question whether there is any likelihood of a general abandonment of the gold standard deserves careful consideration.

It would be idle to deny that the gold standard has become extremely unpopular in most parts of the world during the crisis. The system is blamed by many experts and by the majority of public opinion in this country, as having been the main cause of the crisis. To examine how far this accusation is justified would in itself require a volume. In the author's opinion, the gold standard certainly had an important share in bringing about the crisis. The evil effects of its operations were due, however, to the absence of an adequate gold stock to meet the increased post-war requirements. Most countries had very narrow margins of gold reserve. In particular, the British gold stock was highly inadequate; not only did it preclude any possibility of credit expansion, but every relatively small outflow of gold necessitated measures of credit restriction to safeguard the stability of sterling. This explains why the gold standard has become so extremely unpopular in the country which originated the system, and which, through its extensive interest in gold production, has most to lose by its abolition.

The idea of abandoning the gold standard and replacing it by a system of managed currency is not new. Proposals to that effect were made by various prominent experts long before the crisis. The gold standard was denounced as unscientific, barbarous, and old-fashioned. From a strictly economic point of view the experts who hold such views are doubtless right. Where their doctrines fail is that they leave the human factor out of account. The habit of mankind to prefer gold to anything else as a preserver of values is some thousands of years older than the system of the gold standard. It would in all probability survive the abolition of that system. The degree to which the public in most countries has reverted to gold-hoarding during the crisis gives an idea how deep-rooted the instinct is in human nature. Ninety people out of a hundred who hastened to acquire gold when conditions became uncertain did not argue the case for and against gold as an investment; they simply followed an instinct which is stronger than any influence of economic teaching.

It is customary among radical economists to denounce this primitive instinct as the major obstacle to a rational solution of the monetary problem by the adoption of a scientific currency. In reality, the public's instinctive preference for gold is extremely useful for mankind. It is a great blessing that there is one commodity which is universally accepted without limitation in return for goods and services. If there were no such commodity it would be the duty of economists and statesmen to do their utmost to invent one, as, in its absence, it would be extremely difficult for the nations to accumulate reserves against a rainy day. There would be no shock-absorber to assist Governments in the task of tiding their countries over spells of adverse conditions.

Fortunately, we are in a position to support the case for gold with a concrete example. The experience of Germany during the second half of 1934 provides an example of the conditions that would exist in a world without a gold standard. If gold were to be universally demonetised, every country would be in exactly the same position as Germany is as a result of the depletion of her gold stock. Were any country, owing to a bad harvest, or for whatever other reasons, unable to export, it would immediately have to cut down its imports to a corresponding degree, since it would not possess that universally acceptable commodity—gold—with which to replace its commodity exports and thereby survive one or two bad seasons.

It may be objected that the international credit apparatus would tide countries over their temporary difficulties and that international lending would enable them to cover their trade deficits. It may well be asked, however, whether the absence of gold reserves would in any way facilitate international borrowing. The answer is most emphatically in the negative. Would any conscientious broker advise his client to subscribe to a loan by a country which had no gold reserves, and which would, in consequence, have to default during the first bad year? Admittedly it is possible for the debtor to borrow an amount sufficient for maintaining the interest service. That was actually done in the past by many countries, though the result was not exactly encouraging for investors. In the absence of a gold reserve, however, investors would be asked to lend on the tacit understanding that in the first bad year the debtor would inevitably have to resort to such additional borrowing. Having no gold reserve to fall back upon, the debtors would have to choose between defaulting or borrowing on highly onerous terms, which again would depreciate the capital value of their earlier issue.

Nor would bankers be keen on granting short-term credits to countries without gold reserves, since such credits would become frozen as soon as conditions in the debtor country changed slightly for the worse. It may be objected that even under the gold standard a major crisis leads to an embargo on gold exports and places creditors in exactly the same unenviable position as if there were no such thing as a gold standard. The difference is, however, that under the gold standard it would take an exceptionally severe crisis, or a series of bad years, to produce the effect which would be produced, in the absence of the gold standard, by a moderate deterioration of conditions in a single bad year.

Advanced currency reformers may well denounce the public for its foolish preference for gold. Even if we were to admit that this preference is unscientific, unjustified and unreasonable, we ought to thank our lucky stars for the "foolishness" of the public. It is of immense advantage to a country to possess a commodity which it can export to any other country at any time without difficulties. In given circumstances it is the possession of that "scrap iron" of no social utility that staves off starvation.

We must not fall, however, into the common error of monetary specialists by allowing our wish to be the father to our thought. If we were to depend for our anticipation that the gold standard will be maintained on the hope that the world's statesmen will realise how useful the system is, the basis of our conclusion would be very uncertain indeed.

In examining the prospects of the price of gold, what matters is not what *should* happen with regard to the gold standard but what *will* happen. It is safe beyond doubt to take it for granted that the gold standard will never be universally abandoned. Those countries with large stocks of gold, such as France, Holland, Switzerland, etc., would not think of replacing the gold standard with a managed currency in which gold plays no part. Although the United States may modify the system considerably—possibly by the inclusion of silver, or by other devices—it is certain that she will not discard her gold stock. In this world the right thing is done very often for wrong reasons; the gold standard will be retained, not because a majority of people are convinced that it is to the interest of mankind to do so, but largely because those countries possessing large gold stocks will work in favour of its retention. As far as Great Britain is concerned, although the actual gold stocks in her possession are much smaller than those of France or the United States, vested interests working in favour of retaining the system are none the less strong. After all, the British Empire produces 70 per cent of the world's current gold output. The Union of South Africa is the world's largest gold-producer, and Canada occupies second place. Gold-production is an important source of the national income of Australia, India, Rhodesia, British West Africa, and other Crown Colonies. The gold hoards of India run into hundreds of millions of pounds; the value of unmined gold which sooner or later will be produced and sold amounts to milliards of pounds.

In such circumstances it is strange that the attacks on the gold standard and the demand for its complete demolition should come from Great Britain, while countries with little or no gold production of their own cling to the gold standard in face of the British attacks. The British attitude towards the gold standard, therefore, amounts to an attempt to persuade our customers that one of our principal products is not worth buying. Even if gold were really as worthless as the opponents of the gold standard in Great Britain try to make out, surely it is not for us to put the buyers of gold wise about it. If they are foolish enough to supply the British Empire with real goods and services in return for the yellow metal, let them do so by all means.

Strangest of all, the anti-gold campaign is conducted from quarters which have always claimed to be the supreme defenders of Imperial interests. Does Lord Beaverbrook think that, in being instrumental to the abolition of the gold standard—which is one of the objects pursued systematically by his group of newspapers—he would render a valuable service to the Union of South Africa, to his native land Canada, and other parts of the Empire? Or is he simply unaware of the importance of gold production in the economic systems of the various Dominions and Colonies? Apart altogether from the economic aspects of the problem, does he realise its political implications? If Great Britain were definitely to abandon the gold standard it would sever the most important link that ties the Union of South Africa to the British Empire. General Hertzog, who controls the present destinies of that Dominion, has no love for Great Britain. The reason why he changed his policy and concluded an alliance with General Smuts was because he realised the extent to which the destinies of the system of the gold standard and the prosperity of South African gold production are in the hands of Great Britain. Were we to abandon the gold standard, there would be nothing to prevent the Union from severing completely its association with the Empire. Nor would the anti-gold policy in any way help Great Britain's relations with Canada. As for India, a reduction in the value of its immense gold hoards would inflict severe hardship on the population; and economic depression breeds discontent with the existing régime. The reason why violent opposition to the British rule in India has abated during the last three years is that economic conditions have improved; and one of the main factors in this improvement has been the rise in the price of gold. Thus, were Lord Beaverbrook's anti-gold campaign to be successful, it would not only destroy a large portion of the wealth of the Empire but would encourage in more than one direction the disruptive forces which are at work.

Fortunately for the British Empire, for mankind as a whole and, not least, for Lord Beaverbrook himself, there is not the remotest chance of his anti-Empire crusade succeeding. It is the declared policy of the National Government ultimately to restore the gold standard. The fact that the gold reserve of the Bank of England has been increased substantially and that the Exchange Equalisation Account is endeavouring to accumulate a substantial gold stock of its own is sufficient to indicate the trend of British official policy. Nor is there any likelihood of a fundamental change in this respect under a Labour Government. While a great deal is being said at present in Socialist quarters against the gold standard, once the Labour Party assumed the responsibility of office, its attitude on the question of principle would not differ materially from that of the present Government. Indeed, Great Britain could no more afford to abolish the monetary use of gold than she could the use of coal or of Lancashire textile products. Those Englishmen who advocate the definite abolition of the gold standard are cutting the tree under themselves, just as they would do if they were foolish enough to advocate the use of oil instead of coal, or the purchase of Japanese textiles instead of British.

Apart altogether from considerations of vested

interest, the technical difficulties of demonetising gold would in themselves be sufficient to discourage any inclination on the part of Governments to make such a decision. When, during the last quarter of the nineteenth century, silver was demonetised by a large number of countries, it was a relatively simple matter. All they had to do was to sell silver and buy gold. It would be interesting to know against what the opponents of the gold standard would propose to sell the accumulated gold stocks. If Great Britain, for instance, were anxious to get rid of her gold reserve, would she ship it to France and the United States and acquire franc and dollar balances in exchange? In doing so she would assume the risk of exchange depreciation. Would she accept goods in return for the gold? In doing so she would inflict heavy losses upon her home production. Would she be prepared to lend it to countries anxious to increase their gold reserve? As it is, the indebtedness of the world to Great Britain is excessive and in all probability will have to be scaled down by agreement. In such circumstances, to grant additional loans to the debtors would amount to giving them presents.

If the abandonment of the gold standard by one single country with a relatively moderate gold stock presents such problems, the difficulties in the way of its universal abandonment are easy to imagine. The only way Central Banks could then get rid of their gold would be by issuing it to the public in the form of coins. In that case, however, there would be two kinds of money in circulation and it is not difficult to guess which the public would prefer. In times of difficulty, the coins would go to a premium, and this would undermine confidence in the inconvertible managed currency. The existence of a large monetary circulation over which the authorities have no control would make the management of the currency a most difficult problem.

There remains the possibility of maintaining the gold stocks in the vaults of Central Banks without adding anything to them through new purchases, and of liquidating them gradually, as and when private demand is prepared to absorb it. Even then there would be a likelihood of a strong private demand for hoarding purposes, and privately owned gold stocks might become rivals to the authorities as a potential basis for credit. It is thus evident that the demonetisation of gold would encounter almost unsurmountable technical difficulties. The only way to get rid of the gold stocks without causing complications would be to destroy them or to sink them in the sea. Somehow, it is difficult to visualise the thrifty Frenchman, the dollar-worshipping American, the business-like Dutchman, and the rest of them, doing such a thing. If only those five or six countries which have large gold stocks, and could not afford to destroy them, remained on a gold basis, it would be sufficient to secure a permanent demand for the gold supplies of the rest of the world.

Admittedly, if the return to the gold standard in circumstances similar to those existing before 1931 were the only alternative to managed currency, the outlook would be very grim indeed. It is, fortunately, possible to restore the gold standard in circumstances which provide an adequate safeguard against the recurrence of the evils attached to its application before the crisis. We shall deal with this way out in later chapters.

CHAPTER IX

CENTRAL BANKS' GOLD PURCHASES

HAVING reached the conclusion that the gold standard will not be abandoned, the next step is to consider whether it is likely to be modified in such a way as to affect the price of gold. It is sometimes suggested that, although most countries may return sooner or later to the gold standard, the system to be adopted will not provide for an unlimited absorption of gold at an officially fixed price. Should this be the case, it is suggested that the hoarded gold would have to be sold in the open market; and as, with the return of confidence, the demand for hoarding or for private purposes would probably be exceeded by the amount of dishoarding, the market price of gold would decline to well below the official price.

This question, which we propose to examine in this chapter, is not to be confused with the broader problem of the probable relation between total gold requirements and supply. For the moment we are only concerned with the immediate situation following upon the return to the gold standard. Whether in the long-run, in the course of the operation of the system, the supply of gold will be found to be excessive or deficient is a question that we shall consider in later chapters.

The author's defence of the gold standard in the last chapter might easily convey the impression that he is an adherent of the orthodox monetary school. This, however, is by no means the case. While he is convinced that the gold standard should not be abandoned and will not be abandoned, he holds equally strong views about the necessity for drastic modifications in the principles and working of the system compared with pre-war, and particularly pre-crisis, days. He is convinced that the gold standard will never be restored in this country in the form in which it operated before 1931. To his mind, it is simply unthinkable that the little game of the bank rate, so dear to the hearts of *laissez-faire* economists and orthodox central-bankers, will ever be restored. It is unthinkable that on a fine Thursday morning at the meeting of the Court of the Bank of England, twenty-six merchant bankers should be once more in a position to decide that, since the Bank has lost a few million pounds of gold, a few hundred thousands of workmen should be thrown out of employment through an increase of the bank rate and restriction of credit, so as to readjust the monetary position. The system in which bank-rate changes and other decisions affecting the industrial situation were made by the Bank of England without even consulting the Treasury, and without considering anything but the immediate technical position of the Bank, will never return again. The public knows too much about it and is most unlikely to put up with it. For this reason, it may be taken for granted that, when this country returns to the gold standard, the system adopted will be different in many ways from the one which operated before the crisis. It is also reasonable to assume that other countries on a gold basis will follow the British lead, as they usually do in matters of monetary system.

The question which concerns us from the point of view of the future price of gold is whether, under the modified system, Central Banks will be under legal obligation to buy and sell gold freely at a fixed price. Is it conceivable that they may adopt the rule of operating only in certain specified types of cases, or only if and when it suits their purpose? The adoption of such rules would not be entirely without precedent. In Holland, for instance, the Central Bank is only prepared to sell gold if it is proved that the buyer withdraws it for the purpose of selling it to another Central Bank on a gold basis. Germany went a step further and maintained the stability of the exchange in relation to gold exclusively by official selling of gold as and when the Reichsbank considered it necessary. It has to be noted that, in the case of both Holland and Germany, the Central Banks were always prepared to buy any gold offered to them for sale at the official buying price, without asking any questions as to the nature of the transaction. It was only when it came to selling that the said restrictions were applied.

It is, nevertheless, conceivable, though not probable, that under a modified system such restrictions may apply to both the buying and selling of gold by Central Banks. Should that be the case, hoarders would not always be in a position to dispose of their gold by selling it to the Central Banks at the official buying price. This would unquestionably mean that the statutory buying price would not constitute the minimum limit below which the market price of gold could not possibly fall. The gold which is not taken by the Central Bank would have to be disposed of in the market, presumably, at a lower rate. It is extremely unlikely, however, that the discrepancy between the open-market price and the official price would be considerable and that hoarders should suffer heavy losses in consequence. If the Bank of England should at a certain moment be unwilling to buy the gold offered for sale, in all probability there would always be some other Central Bank which would be prepared to take it. In that case the extent of the holder's loss would be limited to the cost of transport to the country concerned.

It is extremely improbable that at any given moment all Central Banks would refuse to buy gold. Should, however, such a situation arise, the London market price of gold would fall considerably below the official buying price. The reason that such a situation is most unlikely to be allowed to develop is that, in that case, sterling would break away from gold. It would appreciate in terms of gold, which is the last thing the authorities would wish to see happen. After all, a return to the gold standard implies the maintenance of the fluctuation of sterling in terms of gold within reasonably narrow limits. Possibly the limits might be widened to, say, 5 per cent, as is suggested by Mr. J. M. Keynes. It is most unlikely, however, that under any gold standard system, however modified, the monetary authorities would allow a really wide discrepancy to develop between the official and the unofficial price of gold. This being the case, it is immaterial whether or not the Central Bank is under absolute statutory obligation to buy an unlimited quantity of gold at a fixed price. In order to maintain the stability of sterling in terms of gold, the Bank of England would have to take up any excessive market supplies which would otherwise cause a fall in the market price. Whether it took them up through the automatic working of the system, or whether it maintained the stability of the price by open-market purchases at its convenience, is a matter of detail which is not particularly important from the point of view of the future price of gold.

In the author's opinion, this whole question is of purely academic interest, for he is convinced that in practice all Central Banks will be as keen buyers of gold after the return to the gold standard as they were in the past. This will be the case, at any rate, during the early period after the restoration of the gold standard. Should the operation of this system lead, in the long-run, to such a degree of *embarras de richesse* as to cause grave inconvenience, it is conceivable that the system would then be revised. Personally, the author does not believe that there would be a glut of gold, but this could only be ascertained in the course of experience. It is reasonable to assume that the new system would be given a chance for a sufficiently long period to enable all hoarders of gold to unload their holdings should they wish to do so.

There remains the question whether the gold standard would be conducted in the form suggested by Professor Irving Fisher and Professor Warren. The idea of an elastic gold standard under which the price of gold would be changed from time to time was at one time very popular in Washington, but President Roosevelt has since discarded it. It has never been popular among responsible statesmen outside the United States, so that its adoption is extremely unlikely. It is, on the other hand, possible, though not probable, that the parities fixed on the return to the gold standard would not be considered absolutely final. It is conceivable that the Governments would agree upon experimental parities, reserving themselves the right to alter them should it prove necessary. It is also possible that the general conception about the sacrosanct character of the parities might change. Many people are in favour of stabilising sterling, provided that the parities chosen will not be regarded as something absolutely unalterable and their defence will not be considered the supreme task of the nation in any circumstances and at every sacrifice. At the same time, once the parities decided upon were adopted and had been in operation for some time, there would doubtless be strong opposition to any idea of another change unless absolutely unavoidable. If the new parities were ever changed at all, it would be in a downward and not in an upward direction, which means that the price of gold would be raised but not lowered. For it is always easier to defend the parities against an appreciation of the exchange than against a depreciation. It is in order to safeguard ourselves against the latter possibility that the author is strongly in favour of a drastic devaluation of sterling which would widen the "safety margin". An excessive influx of gold would not be a major disaster in any circumstances. The surplus could always be sterilised if the authorities did not want it to affect the volume of currency and credit. It is from the effects of an efflux that we have to safeguard ourselves by playing for safety in stabilising the currency at a low level. The ideal state of affairs is to have a sufficiently large stock of gold not to have to worry about any passing drop in the reserve ratio.

The author's views in this respect are by no means shared by everybody. According to one school, in the event of the stabilisation of sterling and other currencies at a low level, there is every likelihood of a glut of gold, which would prove in the long-run embarrassing, and which would, sooner or later, call for steps to correct the situation through raising eventually the gold value of sterling and of other currencies, so as to check the excessive inflow. The author believes there is no such danger. In any case, the orthodox quarters which might be dissatisfied with inflationary tendencies due to a glut of gold are too conservative to propose to reopen the question of parities, once they are settled with our return to the gold standard. The argument is, however, worth examining, and we propose to discuss it in the next chapter.

CHAPTER X

THE DEMAND FOR GOLD

A GOOD deal has been said in the Press lately about the likelihood of a glut of gold after the stabilisation of currencies. It has been pointed out that, if supplies exceed the requirements of the Central Banks, the price of gold will inevitably fall. This conception is based on an obvious error of fact. Currency stabilisation implies that Central Banks are prepared to buy and sell gold in unlimited amounts, with the consequence that an excessive supply of the metal would not in itself provoke a fall in the price below the official buying figure. If Central Banks are under legal obligation to take up any amount of gold offered to them at a fixed price, then nothing can reduce the price beneath that figure. Even if Central Banks are not under legal obligation to buy the gold offered to them, but are merely anxious to prevent an appreciation of their currencies in terms of gold, a substantial fall in the price of gold through excessive supply would be impossible. In both cases a glut of gold would merely cause an abnormal increase in the reserves of Central Banks, while the price would remain unaffected.

It may be argued, perhaps, that the persistent increase of gold reserves to abnormal figures might induce Governments to change the parities so as to discourage the influx. As we pointed out in the last chapter, this is most unlikely to happen. It is, nevertheless, well worth while to examine the degree of probability of such an embarrassingly persistent influx of gold.

The extent of the Central Banks' gold requirements after stabilisation depends upon a large number of factors. Some of them tend to reduce requirements, while others tend to increase them. A most important factor which will tend to reduce requirements will be, in all probability, the adoption of a reformed system of gold standard, which will be more economical in the use of gold. The post-war system was much more economical than the pre-war system; gold coins were no longer issued, so that practically all monetary gold became gradually concentrated in the hands of the Central Banks. Withdrawal of gold for internal purposes was discouraged unless it served industrial requirements. Above all, the adoption of the gold exchange standard by a large number of countries reduced monetary requirements of the metal to no slight extent. In this respect the crisis reversed the trend of development, as it destroyed the chances of the gold exchange standard becoming popular. A number of Central Banks suffered heavy losses on their foreign exchange reserves, and this induced them to convert all their foreign balances into gold. At present very few Central Banks hold more foreign exchange than necessary for their immediate requirements. Possibly the stabilisation of currencies may improve the situation in this respect, but it is unlikely that the application of the gold exchange standard will ever attain the proportions which it attained before 1931. Indeed, in some countries legislation has been passed to prevent Central Banks from holding any foreign exchange as part of their note cover.

It may be taken for granted that after stabilisation

no country will issue gold coins for circulation, and that most Central Banks will not pay out gold for internal purposes other than industrial requirements. In this respect the rules will probably be more strict than before the crisis. The idea is that in future gold should serve, not as a backing for the note circulation but for settling international balances. Accordingly, the fiction of maintaining the gold reserve as note cover would no longer be kept up. The declared object of the gold stock would then be to maintain the international stability of the currency, which, for internal purposes, would be an inconvertible managed currency secured by a gold reserve.

The reason why radical economists are desirous of divorcing note issue from gold stock altogether is that they are afraid that any fluctuation in the gold stock would otherwise cause corresponding fluctuations in the volume of currency and credit. This was the case in the past and this will doubtless be the case again, unless stabilisation is arranged in circumstances which secure ample safety margins of gold reserve. If devaluation and the acquisition of dishoarded gold should raise the reserve ratio to well above immediate requirements, then there is no reason whatever why fluctuations in the gold reserve within the range of even 20 to 30 per cent should in themselves necessitate any expansion or restriction of credit. Other reasons may present themselves for credit expansion or restriction, but an influx or an efflux of gold would not interfere with credit policy. The idea of a managed currency with a strong gold backing would thus materialise. Gold would be there to inspire confidence, but its fluctuations would not interfere with the course of monetary policy, which could thus be determined in accordance with the broader interests of production and consumption.

Although the adoption of such a system would reduce the requirements of gold for internal purposes, it would not reduce the requirements of Central Banks. For it is only on the assumption that there is an ample margin that such a system of managed gold standard could operate satisfactorily. The adoption of a managed gold standard would not materially affect the demand for gold by Central Banks. On the other hand, the adoption of bimetallism would reduce requirements in the long-run, as they would partly be met by the accumulation of silver supplies. As things are, however, there is not much likelihood of bimetallism being adopted. Scarcity of gold supplies would alone justify such a change. The probability is that after the stabilisation of currencies there will be adequate gold supplies available, provided that currencies are stabilised at a sufficiently low level.

It is possible that a number of countries which were on the gold standard before the crisis will not restore that system—at any rate, not for some years to come. As, however, most of these countries would probably be of minor importance, this would make but little difference to the total requirements of Central Banks. It is sometimes suggested that international co-operation might reduce the gold requirements of Central Banks. We have seen that before the crisis all the efforts made to that end produced little or no result; the hopes attached to the activities of the Bank for International Settlements did not materialise. There is no reason to expect that it would be otherwise after the stabilisation of currencies. Economic nationalism coupled with political distrust will discourage any tendency towards close international co-operation in the monetary sphere. The realisation of the idea of an international gold reserve, or of a redistribution of the world's gold stocks by international agreement, is more remote than ever. There is no reason to expect any reduction of gold requirements on account of such developments.

On the other hand, there may be some natural contraction in gold requirements as a result of the lower volume of foreign trade and foreign lending compared with pre-crisis days. Possibly currency stabilisation may lead to a recovery from the low level to which international trade and international lending has declined during the crisis. The author is convinced, however, that it will be a long time before the volume of 1925–1930 is reached again. This factor may tend to reduce the actual gold requirements of Central Banks, but the necessity for wider margins will remain. Notwithstanding the lower volume of foreign trade and foreign lending, balances which are to be offset by gold shipments are likely to fluctuate within wider limits than before the crisis.

The adoption of international Exchange Clearing to take the place of transfers through the foreign exchange market would, of course, considerably reduce the gold requirements of Central Banks. It is probable that during the period of instability the number of bilateral Exchange Clearing agreements will continue to increase. It is even possible that international Exchange Clearings may eventually be adopted. It is unlikely, however, that the system will be retained after the stabilisation of currencies. Although, in the author's opinion, it is the rational system and is in accordance with the trend towards planned economy, it is more than probable that the world will make another attempt to revert to *laissez-faire* as soon as the present state of emergency is past. International Exchange Clearing will come to stay sooner or later, but not until a crisis of even greater severity than the one experienced during the last few years has made the world realise that it will have to plan or perish.

It is sometimes suggested that gold requirements will be reduced through the abolition of private arbitrage. Doubtless the shipment of gold by private individuals involves a certain degree of wasteful use, for it happens sometimes that purely temporary tendencies give rise to gold movement in both directions. The extent of such waste is, however, negligible, for the amount of gold in transit, which is not included in the reserves of any Central Bank, seldom exceeds a few millions of pounds at a time. If private arbitrage is abolished, which is by no means a foregone conclusion, the reduction of requirements thereby achieved will be very small.

There are doubtless a number of Central Banks which have enough gold for their purpose. From a purely monetary point of view, neither the United States nor France, Switzerland, Holland, nor Belgium, would have to buy more gold. It is possible, however, that France, at any rate, will be anxious to increase her gold stock further in view of the possibility of another war. Nor will she be the only country anxious to accumulate a war chest. There will be, moreover, a large number of Central Banks desirous of increasing their gold stocks for monetary considerations. Several of them have depleted their gold reserves. The Reichsbank, for instance, has spent its gold stock almost completely, and it will doubtless spare no effort to replenish its reserves. The same may be said to hold good to a less degree for the Central Banks of various Danubian States and Balkan States. Nor will Italy want to be left behind in this international contest of gold accumulation. It is the ambition of Signore Mussolini that Italy should be considered in every way as a first-rate Power. While there is little chance of her competing with France regarding her gold reserve, she will doubtless endeavour to reduce the discrepancy between the two countries.

Among the countries outside Europe, Japan is likely to make efforts to recover the gold she lost before and since the suspension of the gold standard. Monetary considerations apart, it is to her interest for political reasons to possess a strong gold reserve. There is a fair possibility that China might adopt the gold standard, which would increase the world's total monetary requirements for gold to a considerable extent. In Latin America several Governments are likely to endeavour to replenish their gold stocks after stabilisation.

Last, but by no means least, the monetary authorities of Great Britain and the British Empire will in all probability be among the potential buyers of gold. It is unthinkable that this country should ever attempt to stabilise sterling with such inadequate gold reserves as she possessed after the war. Events have proved the recommendation of the Cunliffe Report—which estimated the gold reserve requirements of Great Britain at £150 million—to have been hopelessly wrong. The Macmillan Committee estimated the minimum reserve requirement at £200 million, but its conclusions were reached before the crisis. In the light of the experience of 1931, this estimate will have to be revised considerably in an upward direction. Owing to the large amount of foreign balances in London, and the large amount of foreign investments in British securities, this country must possess a very strong gold reserve in order to be safeguarded against a recurrence of the events of 1931. To place the stability of sterling above suspicion, it would be necessary at least to double the amount of gold held at present by the Bank of England.

In other parts of the Empire, monetary gold requirements are also likely to increase as a result of the establishment of Central Banks. Australia has to replenish her depleted gold stock, while Canada has to accumulate a strong gold reserve to secure the independence of her money market from the unduly strong influence of Wall Street.

Allowing for all these conditions, it is reasonable to conclude that the total gold requirements of Central Banks and Governments after currencies are stabilised will be very substantial indeed. Without exaggeration, it may be said that the "gold rush" that will follow stabilisation will be even greater than that experienced between 1925 and 1931.

Taking a long view, the gold requirements of Central Banks will, of course, depend mainly on the tendency of the world price-level. Assuming that prices remain approximately unchanged, the gold rush would subside within a few years. In this respect opinions differ widely; according to one school the devaluation of currencies will not be followed by any material rise in the price-level. Although credit is likely to be expanded considerably, this would not cause prices to rise, for the simple reason that the increase of production would offset the effect of credit extension on the price-level. According to the other extreme school of thought, devaluation would be followed by a spectacular rise in prices, and before very long the safety margins of the gold reserve would be wiped out by the increased requirements due to high price-levels. In the author's opinion, the truth will lie somewhere half-way between the two extremes. It is true that the world's productive capacity of commodities is at present a multiple of actual prediction, so that an extension of credit could increase production almost indefinitely. This does not mean, however, that prices would not rise. Indeed, the only way in which an expansion of credit could increase production would be by bringing about a rise in prices. It is not due to lack of credits that the volume of production has declined to a fraction of total productive capacity. While during the earlier stages of the crisis banks were curtailing credit, at present in most countries the supply of credit is well in excess of demand. Borrowers are not prepared to make use of the credits offered them on favourable terms because there is no adequate demand for their products to justify an increase in their production. What is needed is not a further extension of credit, which would merely increase the volume of idle money, but an increase in the capacity and willingness of consumers to purchase goods. This cannot be brought about by an increase in the volume of credit. It is only by the creation of additional purchasing power that the desired effect could be produced. Additional purchasing power, in turn, would tend to raise prices and the increase of production would, therefore, be preceded and accompanied by a moderate increase in the price-level.

On the other hand, there is no reason to expect that this increase would be sufficient to offset the effects of the devaluation of currencies. The increase in production would keep the rising tendency within relatively moderate limits. In any case, the process of adjusting various categories of prices to the new level of currencies would be a slow one; while wholesale prices would rise quickly, retail prices would lag behind them, and so would wages, real estate values and various other items. The gold requirements of Central Banks are not determined by wholesale prices alone but by an average of wholesale and retail prices, wages, the cost of living and everything that requires the use of money. This average will rise much more slowly than wholesale prices, and it will take decades before it adjusts itself completely to the change. For this reason, while the rise in the price-level will tend to increase the gold requirements of Central Banks, the increase will not be sufficient to wipe out more than a fraction of the safety margin created through the devaluation of currencies. It will, however, materially increase the monetary requirements for gold, especially in later stages when the "gold rush" that is to follow stabilisation has come to an end.

CHAPTER XI

THE SUPPLY OF GOLD

HAVING considered the question of the probable monetary demand for gold after the stabilisation of currencies, let us now turn to the question of the supply from which the requirements are to be satisfied. This is one of the most controversial points in our whole enquiry. The view is held by many people that the return to the gold standard will be followed by a glut of gold entirely without precedent in modern times; that the experience of the period that followed the discovery of the Latin American gold-mines will repeat itself. They base this view on the assumption that before the crisis the supply of gold was more or less adequate, and that after the crisis it will be considerably larger.

Volumes could be written on the controversial question whether the supply of gold before the crisis was sufficient to meet requirements. Some experts maintain that the total volume of monetary gold reserves was not deficient and that the cause of difficulties was merely the maldistribution of that total. While France and the United States had more than their due share of the world's gold stock, most other countries—Great Britain amongst them—had not enough. It is the author's view that, apart altogether from the question of maldistribution, the total of monetary gold supplies was also inadequate. It is true that the Central Banks had succeeded in calling in most of the gold which was in circulation in the form of coins before the war, and that consequently the amount of their gold reserve was in almost every country well above pre-war figures. Notwithstanding this, the increase was not sufficient to keep pace with the enormous expansion of every form of credit that occurred after the war.

Between 1914 and 1931 an immense volume of paper wealth was created in the form of Government debts, private debts, shares, etc. Legally, the gold stock has nothing to do with this fictitious wealth. There is no direct connection between them. Most economists would consider it a heresy for anyone to suggest that because the British public debt is ten times as much as it was before the war, this fact should be considered in determining the amount of gold reserve required by this country. Yet, an increased public debt and every other form of paper wealth constitutes a potential strain on the gold reserve. Before the war the total amount of British Government securities was some £600 million, most of which was held by British nationals; foreign holdings of British Government securities probably never exceeded, say, £20 million to £30 million. To-day they easily run into ten times that amount. Foreigners are in a position to sell at short notice British Government securities amounting to hundreds of millions of pounds, and to sell the sterling thus obtained. Clearly it is the function of the gold reserve to cope with such pressure. It may well be asked how the meagre amount of £130 million of gold reserve this country possessed in 1931 was expected to fulfil that task besides all the other requirements which it had to meet. In the United States and in France there was a similar increase of fictitious wealth in some form. These two countries, at any rate, succeeded in accumulating a sufficiently large gold reserve to cope with the changed situation. The trouble was not that they had too much gold, as most people assumed; it was that other countries did not have nearly enough.

Apart altogether from the material factors which necessitated larger gold holdings, the psychological factor also tended to increase requirements. The pre-war proportions between gold and the volume of fictitious wealth was adequate in the calm and settled conditions prevailing before 1914. Amidst the unsettled conditions that ruled after the war, a much larger proportion would have been necessary as a safeguard against shocks. Instead, the ratio became reduced to a fraction of what it was before the war. The situation was pregnant with possibilities of trouble.

The total gold reserves after the war were inadequate to meet the demand, even if it had been stagnant. In reality, the post-war period experienced a spectacular increase of requirements. This was due in part to the high price-level as compared with 1913; to the increased requirements of consumers that have taken place in most civilised countries since the war; and most of all to the technical improvements in production. All these developments would have necessitated an expansion of credit. On the basis of the existing gold stock, however, there was no scope for any such expansion.

In such circumstances, the author feels, the assumption that the total volume of gold was adequate to meet requirements before the crisis is totally unjustified.

Nor is it justifiable to assume that, after the return

of stability, there will be a spectacular increase in the supply of gold. There are three main sources from which such increase is usually expected to come—the one is the "excessive" gold reserves of the United States and of the countries of the gold group, the other is the private hoards, and the third is an increase in production. In the author's opinion none of these sources is likely to supply gold to a sufficient extent to create a gold surplus.

The opponents of the gold standard are only too ready to assume that holders of large stocks are anxious to get rid of their hoarding, and are terrified of increasing it. This belief is one of the most characteristic examples in which the wish is father to the thought. In reality, neither the United States nor France, nor any of the other gold countries, have shown so far the least sign of being desirous of reducing their gold supplies. On the contrary, each of these countries, in spite of their large stocks, obviously dislikes the idea of losing any gold and equally obviously welcomes every new addition to its reserves. When, in 1933, the outflow of gold from the United States assumed gigantic proportions, the Government suspended the gold standard. Ever since it has concentrated its efforts upon retrieving the gold then lost, whether through purchases abroad or through compelling American hoarders to surrender their hoards. In France the gold standard has so far been maintained, and the Bank of France has, on various occasions, parted with substantial amounts of gold more freely than it was expected. At the same time, the French authorities have used moral pressure to dissuade those desirous of withdrawing gold for internal hoarding. The return of the gold to the vaults of the Bank of France after the improvement of financial conditions this year was greeted with universal joy. There is certainly nothing to indicate that the French authorities consider their present gold-hoarding excessive. Neither the American nor the French authorities are likely to encourage an outflow of gold. On the contrary, both countries are likely to do their utmost to prevent it, and, if possible, to increase their gold stocks. The same may be said to hold good about the other countries with relatively large gold reserves.

It is, of course, possible that the natural tendency caused by an overvaluation of the franc and other gold currencies will result in an outflow of gold from those countries. The chances are, however, that sooner or later, they will remedy the overvaluation by devaluing their currencies. In any case, as things are, the dollar is grossly undervalued, so that whatever gold the countries of the gold group stand to lose will find its way to the United States. Countries with smaller gold reserves will not, therefore, benefit by it. Central Banks anxious to increase their gold reserves will have to meet their requirements out of dishoarding or new production.

The process of dishoarding is likely to be a slow one. It is a mistake to imagine that, as soon as the gold standard is restored in a number of countries, the whole of the £300 million worth of gold which is at present supposed to be hoarded will be surrendered to the Central Banks. It will take time before confidence is sufficiently restored to induce hoarders to part with their gold. It is, in fact, doubtful whether the whole of the hoarded gold will ever be liquidated. The generation that has experienced two periods of currency chaos (that of 1919–1926 and that of 1931–1934) is likely to remain distrustful for a long time to come. The fear of another war is a further strong incentive to the continuation of the hoarding habit after the end of the present period of monetary instability. That factor will be responsible for a desire to hoard, both individually and nationally. Everybody is aware of the advantages of large hoardings during a war, both from the national and the individual standpoint. So long as the international political outlook remains troubled, there is no reason to expect a complete liquidation of gold hoards.

As for current production of gold, this will undoubtedly increase, especially in producing countries other than South Africa. Taxation of the Rand's gold-mining profits is at present such as to encourage the treatment of low-grade ore, with the result that, although Rand profits are greatly increased, the actual production of gold from this, the world's greatest, source is less than previously. The treatment of low-grade ore with the object of lengthening the lives of the mines holds good to a varying extent also for other gold-producing countries. The considerations that influence gold production will be examined in detail in the following chapter. Here let it be sufficient to state that although gold production may tend to be high, its increase will not be nearly as large as many people assume.

The author does not, therefore, share the fear that a glut of gold will materialise. It depends, of course, on the circumstances in which currencies are stabilised. If currencies are devalued to a very large extent, then the nominal amount of the world's monetary gold stock will increase considerably. Even then, it is more than probable that the wide discrepancy between the gold stocks of the United States and the gold group on the one hand, and Great Britain, Central and South-eastern Europe, Japan, etc., on the other, will be levelled not by a reduction in the gold supplies of the former, but by an increase in those of the latter. The problem to be faced will be not how to absorb supplies, but how to satisfy the demand.

CHAPTER XII

THE COST OF PRODUCTION

Up to now we have been examining the factors likely to affect the price of gold. We now propose to examine the question of the prospects of gold-mining shares. The tendency of these shares depends to a large extent upon the price of the metal. There are, however, many other factors which influence the market value of gold-mining shares individually and collectively. We are not concerned with the factors that concern the profits and capital value of any individual company. They vary in merit very widely, and range from the well-established concern of proved value to the speculative venture and shady promotion whose sole gold assets consist of the samples they procure for the benefit of their victims. The discussion of this aspect of the question of gold shares is outside the scope of this book. We propose to confine ourselves to tendencies which affect the prospects of good class gold-mining companies in general. Nor does the author feel qualified to express an opinion as to whether at their present market price, these gold shares are undervalued or overvalued on the basis of the existing gold price. As he is convinced that the price of gold will rise further, he holds the view that, even if the gold-mining shares were overvalued at present, the rise in the price of the metal would amply justify their present price.

The holding of gold-mining shares in preference to hoarding the metal presents several obvious advantages. While gold-hoarding is expensive, the holding of gold-mining shares costs practically nothing; hoarding involves a complete loss of interest, while that class of gold-mining share here being considered pays for its keep by way of dividends. Another advantage of investing in gold-mining shares is that no moral stigma is attached to it. Gold-hoarding is often denounced as an act contrary to public interest—a view which the author does not share. Nobody can, however, find any fault with the holding of gold-mining shares. The worst any extreme opponent of the gold standard can say is that the capital invested in gold-mines produces nothing useful for mankind. At the time of feverish industrial activity when a further extension of production is handicapped by lack of adequate capital resources, such criticism might be worth discussing. At present, however, when the amount of idle capital all over the world runs into milliards of pounds, the funds invested in gold-mines are certainly not missed by mankind, even if it be admitted that gold has no social utility. Yet another advantage of investing in gold-mining shares instead of in gold is that there is no question of gold shares being confiscated by the authorities at an inadequate price. As the author emphasised in Chapter VI., it is extremely unlikely that any such steps would be taken against hoarded gold in Great Britain. The position of shareholders is, however, in this respect, if anything even safer than that of holders of gold deposits.

Against these advantages there are several substantial disadvantages connected with the holding of gold shares. It is possible that they will not appreciate in proportion to the rise in the price of gold. Apart from the question whether such a rise is already discounted, there are two main factors which may prevent an adequate rise in the value of gold shares. It is possible that the cost of production may increase considerably, and that the whole or a large part of the excess profits obtained through the appreciation of gold may be taken away in taxation. Even if the cost of production were to rise in equal proportions to the advance in the price of gold, the value of gold shares should rise in proportion with the price of gold. For, if the cost of production and the market price of the products rise in identical proportion, the percentage of profit remains unchanged. In reality, the chances are that the cost of production will not increase to anything like the extent of the rise in gold.

The cost of production depends upon the tendency of the world price-level, and especially upon that of prices in the producing countries. In addition, influences peculiar to the gold-mining industry are also liable to affect it. As far as factors of a general nature are concerned, they are not likely to cause a rapid rise. As we pointed out in earlier chapters, although a rise in wholesale prices following upon devaluation may safely be anticipated, it will be neither rapid nor complete. Thus if—for the sake of argument—sterling is stabilised at 10s. and the London price of gold is fixed at 169s. 8d., it does not follow that the price-level will rise by 100 per cent. It is doubtful if it would rise even 50 per cent, judging by the American experience of 1933–1934. It will take several years before devaluation produces its full effect on world prices. The same may be said to hold good in regard to the price-level in South Africa. If the rise in wholesale prices is slow and incomplete, this will be the case to an increasing degree for retail prices, the cost of living and wages in general. They always lag behind the movement of wholesale prices and there is no reason to suppose that on this occasion it would be otherwise.

It is certain that the time-lag will favour producers for many years, and that the discrepancy between the rise in the price of gold and the rise in wages will favour them permanently. In this respect it is characteristic that although the South African gold producers have had the benefit of higher gold prices ever since the end of 1932 when the Union of South Africa suspended the gold standard, there has not been any material rise in the cost of production. Wages are substantially the same as two years ago, although the mining companies have made certain concessions in the form of improved working conditions and the institution of further social welfare measures.

It is not possible, naturally, to form any general opinion about the prospects of gold-mining taxation in each and every gold producing country. In the case of South Africa, where the scale of taxation is perhaps the most onerous, there does not seem to be any likelihood of an increase in the future. It is true the Governments in gold-producing countries may be desirous of benefiting to an extensive degree by the increase of gold-mining profits caused by the monetary measures they have taken. Indeed, there seems to be a conception developing which claims that the Government is entitled to the surplus value of gold—whether in the form of Central Banks deposits, private hoards, or newly mined gold—created through the depreciation or devaluation of the national currency.

As far as the gold stocks of Central Banks are concerned, this conception is doubtless justified. The gold reserve of a country is not the private property of its

Central Bank; the latter only acts as custodian for the nation. This idea is clearly expressed in the separation of the Banking Department from the Issue Department in the returns of the Bank of England. In practice, in several countries, when the currency was devalued after the war, the rise in the bookkeeping value of the gold reserve was credited to the Government. This principle has been established beyond doubt, and it is a foregone conclusion that in every country the Government will have the benefit of the revaluation of the gold reserve.

The situation is totally different in the case of private gold hoards and newly mined gold. In this case, the gold constitutes private property and is held at the risk of its owners. In the case of gold reserves of Central Banks, the Governments stand any loss that may arise through their monetary measures, and it is therefore reasonable that they should benefit by the profit. Losses on gold hoards and newly mined gold would have to be borne by their owners and it would be absurd if the Government were to claim any surplus value that might arise. Moreover, in the case of Central Banks the ownership of gold remains the same, while in the case of hoards and newly mined gold the ownership may change innumerable times. Conceivably the last owners acquired the gold or the gold-mining shares at a price which already fully discountered the surplus; indeed, it is possible that the price of gold will be stabilised below its maximum level, in which case the actual owners of hoarded gold and gold-mining shares who acquired their property at top prices, would suffer losses. It would be unfair and unjust to claim from them a "surplus" which was in reality obtained by previous owners.

There is little likelihood of this confiscatory principle being adopted concerning gold-mining companies. It is true that they are subject to heavy taxation, but so far the object of such taxes as have been adopted has not been to deprive gold-mining companies of their surplus. The object of the heavy taxation is not to enforce a principle but to balance the budget. Every Government raises its revenue where it thinks there are resources available. The idea of claiming the surplus value on gold other than the reserve of Central Banks is entirely unjustified. After all, it is not only gold that appreciates through the monetary decisions taken by Governments. The chances are that, sooner or later, every commodity will appreciate to a more or less extent. So long, therefore, as the surplus earned through such rise in commodity prices is allowed to remain in private ownership it would be inconsistent to make an exception in the case of gold or gold-mining shares.

Apart altogether from considerations of rights, equity, and consistency, the confiscation of the surplus profits of gold-mining companies would be a mistake, also, from a practical point of view. It is thanks to the wider margin of profits made possible by the rise in the price of gold that gold-mining companies are able to work low-grade ores which would otherwise be neglected. It is obviously in the interests of gold-producing nations that the life of their gold-fields should be thus prolonged, as this benefits the national wealth as well as the actual proprietors.

SUMMARY

Since the subject-matter of this book is necessarily of a highly involved nature, the author has endeavoured throughout to eliminate unnecessary complications. He is aware, nevertheless, that the bewildering array of factors affecting the price of gold puts the memory of his readers to an unduly severe test; and for this reason he has thought it fit to provide a guide enabling his readers to grasp at a glance his conclusions.

For the sake of simplicity, the summary of the main points of the book is arranged in tabular form, showing the causes for any likely or possible changes in the price of gold, if and when the changes are likely to occur, and their probable effect in the short-run and in the long-run.

Cause.	If and When Likely to Happen.	Effect on Price of Gold.	
		In the Short-run.	In the Long-run.
Sterling Depreciates:			
(1) For seasonal causes	Probable in last quarter of year	Temporary rise	. .
(2) Owing to Adverse Trade Balance	Uncertain	Rising tendency	Stabilisation at high figure
(3) Owing to over-lending	Possible	Moderate rise	Uncertain
(4) Owing to policy of Exchange Equalisation Account	Probable	Uncertain	Substantial rise and stabilisation at high figure
(5) Owing to general economic policy (tariffs, restoration of cuts, etc.)	Probable in long-run	Uncertain	Steady rise

Cause.	If and When Likely to Happen.	Effect on Price of Gold.	
		In the Short-run.	In the Long-run.
(6) Owing to political reasons	Certain before General Election	..	Considerable rise
Sterling Appreciates:			
(1) For seasonal causes	Certain in first quarter of year	Temporary fall	..
(2) Owing to an influx of funds	Highly probable in immediate future	Sharp fall	Recovery to old record level
(3) Owing to inflation in United States	Possible	Considerable fall	Recovery to old level
(4) Owing to devaluation of the dollar	Probable	No change	Rise through adjustment of sterling to dollar
(5) Owing to operations of American authorities	Unlikely	Possible fall	Recovery to old level
(6) Owing to resistance of France to adverse trend	Highly probable in immediate future	Sharp fall	Readjustment
(7) Owing to devaluation of franc	Probable in long-run	No effect	Rise in case of depreciation race
(8) Owing to suspension of gold standard by all Countries	Unlikely but possible	Spectacular rise	Stabilisation at very high price
Hoarding Increases:			
(1) Under existing conditions	Possible through flight from franc	Rise in premium	Immaterial
(2) If all countries suspend gold standard	Unlikely but possible	Spectacular rise	Stabilisation at high level
Hoarding Decreases:			
(1) Under existing conditions	Unlikely but possible	Fall in premium	Immaterial
(2) After stabilisation	Probable	..	Price unaffected
Stabilisation by International Agreement	Probable within the next few years	..	Stabilisation at high figure
Stabilisation in absence of International Agreement	Possible in distant future	..	Stabilisation at high figure

Cause.	If and When Likely to Happen.	Effect on Price of Gold.	
		In the Short-run.	In the Long-run.
All countries definitely abandon gold standard	Most unlikely	..	Heavy fall
All countries adopt restricted gold standard			
(1) Central Banks will not buy gold freely	Unlikely	..	Moderate fall from high level
(2) Parities will be subject to changes	Unlikely	..	Price fluctuates

The author holds the view that, on balance, the chances are that after a very moderate rise the price of gold will relapse in the near future. Conceivably by the time this book is published the tide will have already turned; if not, the downward change in the tendency will be imminent. However, the author is convinced that the price of gold will recover to well above its present level of 143s. per ounce. He is equally convinced that the final rate of stabilisation will fix the price of gold at well above its present figure.

Although the gold standard is likely to undergo a reform, Central Banks will continue to be unlimited buyers of gold, for which reason a relapse in its price after stabilisation is out of the question. Once currencies are stabilised, their new parities are not likely to be revised subsequently in such a manner as to cause a fall in the price of gold.

Provided that the rate of stabilisation is fixed at a reasonable level there will be ample margins of gold stocks available. Notwithstanding this, the author does not expect a glut of gold, because he is convinced that whatever supplies are available will be readily absorbed by countries anxious to increase their stocks. In any case he does not expect a spectacular increase in production or the complete dishoarding of the amount of gold hoarded. Gold requirements are likely to increase as a result of a rise in prices, but this rise will not be sufficient to cancel out the surplus created through the devaluation of currencies. It will be gradual and will remain inferior to the rise in the price of gold.

As for gold-mining shares, they will doubtless benefit by the high price of gold notwithstanding high taxation in South Africa and elsewhere and the slow increase in the cost of production that is likely to take place.

Under the new gold standard system, the internal use of gold will probably be reduced to a minimum. The author thinks it unlikely that gold will be formally divorced from note circulation, but in practice much more importance will be attached to providing for the necessities of international fluctuations than to provision for note cover. In any case, the existence of substantial safety margins as a result of the drastic devaluation of currencies will facilitate the working of the system to a larger extent than any possible measures of reform.

The stabilisation of sterling, and most other currencies which are at present off the gold standard, is not likely to take place for at least another year or two. In the meantime the chances are that those currencies at present on a gold basis will either "come off" gold, or, what is much more probable, will be devalued. The success of the coming stabilisation will be less dependent on international co-operation than was the attempt of 1923–1928. For this reason the basis of this stabilisation will be more realistic, and the world will be less exposed to disappointment.

APPENDIX I

GOLD DURING THE CRISIS

BEFORE the suspension of the gold standard in Great Britain the range of the fluctuations of gold in London was limited to the difference between the buying and selling price of the Bank of England. From September 1931 onwards, however, the London gold market experienced very wide movements. In September the price of gold rose from 84s. 11d. to 114s. 9d.; well before the end of the year the record price of 126s. 10d. was reached. The recovery of sterling early in 1932 brought about a decline in the price of gold, which touched 108s. in April. For the rest of the year the price of gold rose most of the time, and in November a new high record was reached at 130s. 8d. as a result of the further depreciation of sterling. During the first quarter of 1933 there was again a declining tendency and in March the price fell back to 121s. 11½d. Following upon the suspension of the gold standard in the United States, the gold value of sterling underwent a gradual depreciation and the price of gold rose again month after month. In October 1933 it touched a new high record at 134s. 8d. Towards the end of that year the flight from the dollar and from the franc caused sterling to improve, so that in December the price of gold declined to 123s. 8d. Early in 1934, following upon the stabilisation of the dollar, the London price of gold rose to 140s., but later in the year it declined, and between March and August moved irresolutely between 134s. and 140s. It was not until September that the previous record was exceeded as a result of the depreciation of sterling, and early in October the price broke all previous records at 143s. 3d.

Apart from temporary fluctuations, the price of gold has had a decidedly upward trend ever since 1931. This was largely the result of the depreciation of sterling, but in addition the price of gold showed almost continuously a premium over the gold exchanges due to the keen demand for hoarding purposes which has been one of the characteristic features of the last three years. At the same time, there was a good deal of dishoarding in Great Britain and British India. In Great Britain, towards the end of 1931, a large number of sovereigns came on the market. Attracted by the high price, people who had held sovereigns since pre-war days sold them to the local jewellers, who in turn disposed of them in the London market. Although no figures are available to indicate the approximate extent of this movement, the quantities of sovereigns sold to London bullion brokers and other large buyers surprised most people. Nobody ever imagined that such large numbers of sovereigns had been retained. A regular market developed in sovereigns and other coins as well as in trinkets and broken gold of every kind. Whereas before the crisis the London gold market was essentially a wholesale market, during the crisis retail business was done in gold on a large scale. Sovereigns and other coins commanded a very good price. They were at a premium compared with bar gold because of the popularity of coins among the hoarding public in France and other Continental countries. Coins are much more convenient for hoarding purposes than bar gold, since it is much easier to dispose of them. For this reason the premium on coins in France rose at one time to about 5 per cent.

Dishoarding in India assumed spectacular dimensions. Until the crisis, India was one of the most important buyers of gold. Even before the war, in 1911–1912, her gold imports amounted to £31 million. This record was beaten during the first post-war year, when the figure exceeded over £36 million, while in 1924–1925 a new high record was established at 55·7 million pounds. From 1931 onwards India began to export gold on a spectacular scale. This was partly due to the unfavourable conditions caused by depreciation, but the movement continued after an economic recovery had set in. The gold came partly from the large hoards of princes and other wealthy people, and partly from the jewels and coins of the population. In September 1931 and March 1933 the amount of gold exported was over £94 million. The outflow continued on a fluctuating scale throughout 1933 and 1934. Most of the gold finds its way through the intermediary of the Bombay dealers to the London market.

Indeed, the London gold market has retained its superiority throughout the crisis. Admittedly, an active market developed in France owing to the hoarding fever of the public. The banks have acquired large stocks, and retail trade in gold has been flourishing. The French market is, however, purely local and does not in any way threaten London's lead in the international field. The London market benefited to a large extent by the transfer of foreign gold hoards to London. While a large number of holders simply deposit their hoards with some London bank or safe deposit company, others make use of their hoardings for arbitrage and speculation. As a result, the gold changes hands frequently and the turnover of the London gold market is now much larger than it was before the crisis. In the old days Tuesday was practically the only active day in the gold market, as the weekly shipments from South Africa arrived in this country on Mondays. On other days of the week the sales were usually very restricted. Since the crisis the gold market has a much larger average turnover on every weekday, for, in addition to the South African gold arrivals, almost every mail-boat from India brings important consignments, and transactions in hoarded gold often amount to considerable figures.

The London gold market is now much more elastic than it was before the crisis. A keen demand results in the increase of the premium of gold on the franc and induces a number of hoarders to sell out and cover themselves by subsequent withdrawals from the Bank of France. Thanks to such transactions in addition to the South African and Indian gold arrivals, the daily turnover in the gold market is seldom less than £500,000. A large part of this is dealt with at the time of the fixing when the official price of gold is decided upon. Since the crisis, however, a very active market has developed after fixing, and very often large amounts change hands at prices which are totally different from the official figure. Another feature of the unofficial gold market is dealing in forward gold, a form of transaction that was practically non-existent before the crisis.

The hoarding of gold has brought the London market a source of income which is by no means negligible. There has never before been such a demand for safe accommodation, which benefits safe deposit companies and banks. Insurance companies also derive considerable benefit from gold-hoarding, since it is essential to insure the gold against various kinds of risks, the liability of banks and of safe deposit companies being limited. The transport of gold is a useful source of profit to shipping agencies and carriers. The loading and unloading of vans containing bar gold has become an everyday sight in the City, providing visible evidence of the increased turnover.

A certain amount of gold is being hoarded for purely speculative purposes; in many cases a transaction is financed with borrowed funds. This practice is considered undesirable by the authorities, and the Clearing Banks have made it a rule not to encourage it by granting loans on the security of gold deposits. Financial houses and foreign bank branches do not, however, follow this rule, especially as, in the absence of an active commercial demand for credit, it is tempting to employ their funds without taking any risk.

The British authorities have from time to time taken an active part in the London gold market. Before the crisis the only occasions when the Bank of England was a buyer of gold were when it acted on behalf of some foreign Central Bank. The "unknown buyer" always operated on account of foreign authorities. During the crisis, however, the Exchange Equalisation Account is believed to have become an important buyer of gold in the London market. In addition to acquiring gold through withdrawals from the Federal Reserve Bank of New York before March 1933 and from the Bank of France since the suspension of the gold standard in the United States, the British authorities are believed to have often increased their stocks out of the supplies available in the open market. They have never pursued, however, a declared gold-buying policy such as has been adopted by the United States authorities. The latter fixed an official gold-buying price in October 1933, which was raised subsequently from $31·36 to $35 per ounce.

The successive increases were as follows:

		$			$
October	25	31·36	November	10	33·20
„	28	31·82	„	11	33·32
„	30	31·96	„	13	33·45
„	31	32·12	„	14	33·56
November	1	32·26	„	25	33·76
„	2	32·36	„	28	33·85
„	3	32·57	„	29	33·93
„	4	32·67	December	1	34·01
„	5	32·84	„	17	34·06
„	8	33·05	January	16	34·45
„	9	33·15	„	31	35·00

It was not until the price of gold had been stabilised at $35 for some weeks that the dollar exchange adjusted itself to its new gold parities. Before January 31, the gold price was ineffective owing to the difficulties of international arbitrage.

In February 1934, following on the stabilisation of the gold price at $35, there were heavy arbitrage shipments from the open market in London and from the Continental Central Banks to New York. It was not until the end of February that the dollar adjusted itself to the new gold-buying price and the gold shipments gradually ceased.

International gold movements have been going on throughout the crisis on a large scale. Towards the end of 1931 and the first half of 1932, the repatriation of dollar balances in the form of gold by Continental Central Banks resulted in a heavy flow of gold to Europe. During the third quarter of that year the movement became reversed, but towards the end of the year and the beginning of 1933 the flight from the dollar resulted in a renewed outflow of gold. After the suspension of the gold standard in the United States, there were no particularly heavy gold movements until President Roosevelt's gold policy provoked a flow of gold from Europe to the United States.

France experienced a heavy influx of gold throughout 1931

and 1932, but in 1933 and early in 1934 the flight from the franc caused heavy withdrawals on various occasions. During the second and third quarters of 1934, however, the Bank of France more than recovered its losses through purchases from the Exchange Equalisation Account and through an influx from the other countries of the gold group. The countries which had to liquidate a large proportion of their gold reserves included Japan, Germany, and some Latin American States. As a result of these movements, the much-criticised maldistribution of gold has become further accentuated during the crisis.

APPENDIX II

GOLD PRICE *v.* EXCHANGE RATE

The controversial question whether it is the exchange rate of sterling that determines the London price of gold or *vice versa* deserves more attention than it has hitherto received. Although it may now appear to be of a purely academic nature, a situation may arise in which it would assume considerable practical interest. It is beyond doubt that, in the case of two countries on the gold standard, the ratio between their respective official price of gold determines the exchange rate, which cannot materially depart from the gold points. For the purpose of our enquiry, it is important to make it plain that the main reason why, under the gold standard, an outflow of gold causes a recovery of the exchange while an inflow has an adverse effect, is because the transactions give rise to a buying or selling pressure on the exchange. There are, doubtless, also other channels through which gold movements in normal conditions affect exchanges. Their effect on interest rates tends to influence the international flow of short-term funds; contraction or expansion of credit caused by gold movements may affect the trade balance through their influence on the price-level; there is also the psychological factor, which cannot be overlooked. For the purpose of our enquiry, however, it is essential to bear in mind that under the system of the gold standard the exchange rates are controlled by the official price of gold, because gold is allowed to move in and out freely and in doing so it produces a direct and immediate effect upon the foreign exchange market.

When it comes to the relation of gold parities to exchange rates between a country on the gold standard and another with an inconvertible paper currency, the state of affairs is not quite so simple. According to one school—which includes most of the practical gold and foreign exchange experts—in such cases it is exchange rates that determine the price of gold. This view is not accepted by everybody; another school of thought holds the opinion that gold price and exchange rate affect each other reciprocally. While the movements of the gold exchanges influence the London price of gold, the gold price itself has a certain influence on the exchange value of sterling. According to this theory, strong demand or inadequate supply of gold tends to raise the market price of gold, and this again tends to cause sterling to depreciate. On the other hand, slack demand and excessive supply tend to cause a fall in the gold price and a rise in the exchange value of sterling.

President Roosevelt's gold policy was partly based on such assumption. His advisers believed that in changing the buying price of gold, the exchange value of the dollar would automatically adjust itself to the new price even if no actual business were transacted at that price. The wide discrepancy between the provisional gold parities of the dollar and its actual exchange rates between October 1933 and January 1934 was apt to cast doubt upon the theory. It ought to be borne in mind, however, that it was lack of international contact between the American official price and the free market price of gold that accounted for the discrepancy. But even had President Roosevelt's gold policy been effective in regulating the dollar exchange, it would not have proved that those are right who maintain that the exchange value of sterling depends upon the price of gold in the open market. It is a natural thing that exchange rates should be determined by the relation between the official gold price in two countries. The London market price is not fixed by the authorities, but varies according to the exchange rate, and, to some extent, the supply and demand. It cannot, therefore, be compared with the official gold-buying price as fixed from time to time by the American authorities between October 25, 1933, and January 31, 1934. It bears even less similarity to the statutory gold-buying and selling price under the gold standard. So long as the official price is effective and gold is allowed to flow in and out in unlimited amounts, the exchange cannot depart from its gold parities. But the amount of gold that can be bought or sold in the open market on the basis of the price quoted at any given moment, is limited. For this reason, if the exchange is undervalued compared with its gold parities based on the market price of gold, the discrepancy cannot give rise to a sufficiently large gold outflow to bring about an automatic readjustment. On the contrary, the chances are that, before sufficient gold is purchased for shipment abroad, the price of gold rises, and the gold parities adjust themselves to the exchange rate.

It is not correct to say that under the existing conditions a strong demand for gold in London is capable of causing a depreciation of sterling through raising the price of gold. So long as there is one Central Bank left which parts with gold freely at a fixed selling price, there is no reason whatever why keen demand for gold should affect sterling through its effect on the London market price. All it does is to raise the premium of gold on the franc, and, if this premium reaches a certain limit, gold will be withdrawn from the Bank of France. Conversely, if there is heavy selling of gold, it does not tend to cause sterling to appreciate so long as there is a Central Bank which is prepared to buy the gold at a fixed price. If the London price of gold falls below a certain point, it becomes profitable to ship the gold and sell it to the Central Bank concerned. The existence of an official buying and selling price for gold in a foreign centre sets a limit beyond which the fluctuation of supply and demand is unable to affect the London market price. It is, consequently, unable to affect the sterling rate.

Should a situation arise in which no Central Bank is any longer prepared to buy or sell gold at a fixed price, then there would be no limit to the extent to which supply and demand could affect the London price of gold. There would be a tendency towards fluctuation in the price of gold in accordance with supply and demand. The question is, whether after the suspension of the gold standard in every country, there would be any gold parities at all. The ratio between the London market price of gold and the market price in other countries hardly deserves the name of parity, since neither France nor the United States could provide a good gold market with which

London could maintain regular arbitrage relations, and the markets in Bombay and Shanghai would, of course, be unable to influence sterling in relation to dollar and Continental currencies. Owing to the predominant importance of London as a gold market, the chances are that in such a situation the London price of gold and the exchange rates of sterling would determine to some degree the price of gold in other countries.

It is probable that in the event of the suspension of the gold standard in every country, the British, American, and possibly the French authorities would attempt to regulate the tendency of their exchanges by operating in the gold market on an extensive scale. The question is whether it would prove possible to regulate the exchanges through the fixing of gold prices. Let us assume, for the sake of argument, that the British authorities fixed at a given moment the official buying price of gold at £10 per ounce; that the official buying price of the American authorities on the same day was $50 per ounce, and that of the French authorities Frs. 1000 per ounce. This does not necessarily mean that the exchange rates would fluctuate around $5 per £1 and Frs. 100 per £1 respectively. It is true that, in normal times, the official price of gold determines the exchange rates. The reason for this is, however, that an unlimited amount of gold is capable of flowing from one Central Bank to another, so long as there is a discrepancy between gold prices and exchanges. This condition would not exist after the suspension of the gold standard by all countries. While the monetary authorities of the three countries would be prepared to be buyers of gold to an unlimited extent at a fixed price, they would declare themselves prepared to be sellers of gold at a fixed price to an unlimited extent. Nor are they likely to be offered an adequate amount of gold at their official buying price. For this reason, gold movements provoked by any discrepancy between exchange rates and the "parities" between official gold prices would not be on a sufficiently large scale to cause immediate readjustment. If the British official buying price is £10 and the French official buying price Frs. 1000, gold should go from this country to France so long as the exchange rate is under Frs. 100 per £1 (less shipping costs) and gold should come from France to this country so long as the franc is offered at about Frs. 100 per £1 (plus shipping costs). It is doubtful, however, whether there would be an adequate amount of gold available for arbitrage to readjust the discrepancy in the event of strong buying or selling pressure on the sterling-franc exchange. So long as the authorities are not prepared themselves to sell on demand, the only gold available for arbitrage would be the supply in the free market. While the London market is likely to have ample supplies, the French market would cease to operate altogether for international purposes after the suspension of the gold standard. As in the case of the United States, the export of gold would probably be prohibited in France once the gold standard was suspended. For this reason, while an appreciation of the franc above its provisional parity might cause a gold movement from the London market to the Bank of France, a depreciation of the franc beneath its provisional parity would not be readjusted by any flow of gold from Paris to London. In practice the efforts to regulate exchanges through fixing the buying price for gold would consist of bidding against each other for the supplies in the London market. If the French authorities were to succeed in acquiring the gold, the franc would tend to depreciate, provided that the purchase of gold involved the sale of francs. It is indeed the only way in which the price of gold can affect exchanges, viz. by giving rise to a buying or a selling pressure on the exchange concerned.

Unless the monetary authorities of the various countries are able to secure a substantial amount of gold at their official buying price, that price will not in itself be effective in determining the exchange rates of the national currencies. The amount of gold purchases that are necessary to make the buying price effective depends on the volume of transactions in the foreign exchange market. On a slack day the sale of £100,000 through the purchase of gold would be in itself sufficient to cause a noteworthy depreciation of sterling. On a really active day a much larger amount would be required to make any material difference in the rate. The psychological factor plays a very important part in this respect.

Moreover, it would be a mistake to imagine that every purchase of gold by the monetary authorities of a country would necessarily result in a corresponding increase of selling pressure on its exchange. All depends upon the way in which the seller of gold disposes of the proceeds. If he leaves them in London, then there is no reason whatever why the transaction should cause any weakening of the exchange of the buying country. It is also conceivable that the foreign buyer already possesses the sterling required for the transaction which does not, therefore, involve any new purchase of sterling.

It is to be borne in mind that the effect on sterling of the purchase or sale of gold in London on foreign account—whether under existing conditions or after the suspension of the gold standard by all countries—depends entirely upon the method of acquisition and disposal of the purchase amount. If the foreign purchaser has to acquire sterling to pay for the gold, and the proceeds of the sale are left in London, then the result is an appreciation of sterling. If the proceeds are transferred abroad, the transactions cancel each other out, and on balance there will be no change in the sterling rate. The same is the result if the purchaser of gold draws on his existing sterling balance, and the seller leaves the proceeds of the sale in London. If, on the other hand, the buyer draws on his existing sterling balance while the seller of gold transfers the proceeds abroad, then the transaction results in a depreciation of sterling. It is, therefore, impossible to state how a gold transaction would affect sterling or any other exchange, unless we know the nature of the source from which the purchase price is paid, and the way in which the seller disposes of the proceeds.

It is, obviously, not a matter of simple arithmetic to try to regulate sterling with the aid of fixing an official buying price for gold. At the same time if the gold standard is suspended in every country there is no other possible way of influencing the exchanges, and the authorities would have to revert to gold policy, operated in the London market, as the only weapon, however inadequate, at their disposal. The British authorities, being on the spot, would be decidedly at an advantage in this respect.

Taking a long view, the exchanges would probably tend to adjust themselves approximately to the relation between the official buying price of gold in various countries. Assuming that for some length of time the British official buying price was £10 and the French official buying price Frs. 1000, so long as the sterling franc rate was under 100, the chances are that the British authorities would acquire gold available in this market. In the long run they would be able to acquire a sufficient amount to cause a corresponding depreciation of sterling—all the more so as the fact that sterling is overvalued compared with its provisional gold parity would discourage foreigners from holding sterling balances. If, on the other hand, the ratio between the British and French official buying prices changes frequently, then the sterling franc exchange has no chance to settle down in the vicinity of its provisional parity.

APPENDIX III

THE GOLD PREMIUM

The term "premium" is used in connection with gold in two different senses. Gold is said by some people to be at a premium compared with its statutory buying price of 84s. 10d. or with its statutory selling price of 84s. 11½d. In this sense, if the price of gold is, say, 143s., it is at a premium of 58s. 2d. or 58s. 0½d., according to whether the statutory buying price or selling price is taken as the basis. This premium is sometimes subdivided into "basic" premium and "super-premium." The former represents the difference between the statutory price and the figure at which gold should be if it were quoted strictly on the basis of the current exchange rate of a gold standard currency, *e.g.*, the French franc or the dollar. The super-premium represents the extra price over and above that figure. This discrimination is of little practical interest, since the old statutory buying price is now a matter of history, and there is no reason why any premium should be calculated on that basis. According to a much more convenient conception, the sterling equivalent of the official gold price in France or in the United States on the basis of the actual exchange rate should be regarded as the basic price, and any difference between that figure and the actual London price of gold should be called the premium. Thus, in this sense, the premium is identical with the "super-premium" in the sense indicated above. As by far the most people who deal with gold speak of a premium in the sense of a premium of gold over the franc or the dollar, we propose to use the term henceforth in that sense only.

Simpler as it may be to deal with one single premium instead of a premium plus a super-premium, the subject remains none the less rather involved. For opinions are by no means unanimous about the exact meaning of the word premium, even in this simplified sense. The most popular formula defines premium as a price in excess of the sterling equivalent obtainable by selling it to the Bank of France and realising the francs at the exchange rate quoted in London at the time of fixing the gold price. In this sense, the premium represents the surplus the seller obtains in London, compared with what he would have obtained if he had sold the gold to the Bank of France. The premium does not allow for the cost of transport, insurance, etc. Thus, if the London gold price is announced to contain a premium, it does not necessarily mean that it would be a paying proposition to withdraw gold from the Bank of France and sell it in the London market; apart from any other reasons, there is also the difference between the buying price and the selling price of the Bank of France to be considered. In order that it should be profitable to withdraw gold from the Bank of France for sale in London, the premium must be at least 1s. In the course of the current year, the premium has only risen to such a figure on rare occasions and for brief periods. At one time, in May 1934, it was as high as 1s. 3½d. per ounce. From time to time, the premium declined to a very low figure, although it has never yet given way to a discount. In theory, it is possible that gold should be quoted at a slight discount which would make it worth while for arbitrageurs to buy in the London market and sell it to the Bank of France. In practice this has never happened since the suspension of the gold standard, and is not likely to happen until considerable progress has been made towards the restoration of confidence.

Under prevailing conditions, the gold points are represented by the premium and the discount at which it becomes profitable to ship gold to and from Paris. As far as the dollar is concerned, in theory there is a possibility for the gold export point to operate, since the United States authorities are prepared to buy gold at a fixed price. The gold import point may or may not operate, as the United States authorities are under no legal obligation to sell gold for shipment abroad, and it is doubtful whether licence would be granted for shipment to a country not on a gold basis. For this reason, the premium of gold on the dollar is much less important than its premium on the franc.

Let us now examine the factors that determine the changes in the premium of gold. To some extent, this premium is influenced by the tendencies of the basic price of gold, but this is a secondary factor. The basic price of gold depends on the sterling-franc rate; it rises whenever sterling depreciates and falls whenever sterling recovers. As the predominant majority of buyers and sellers of gold are residents in countries of the Gold Bloc, an increase in the price of gold through a depreciation of sterling in terms of francs is of no advantage to them. They can, it is true, benefit by the rise of gold without losing an equal amount through a depreciation of sterling, if they cover the forward exchange. In that case, however, they are no longer safeguarded against a depreciation of their own currencies. Thus, the prospects of a depreciation of sterling does not induce many capitalists in the gold countries to buy gold in London. Conceivably it might induce jewellers in Great Britain to cover their requirements, but their demand is an insignificant fraction of the turnover. If the public in this country were in the habit of hoarding gold, the tendencies of sterling would be a most important factor in determining the premium. As it is, possibly residents in some countries of the sterling group may be induced to buy gold when sterling tends to depreciate.

On various occasions a rise in the premium on gold has taken place while the basic price was falling through an appreciation of sterling, while the premium declined simultaneously with a rise in the basic price through the depreciation of sterling. This apparently anomalous state of affairs is easily explained. Whenever sterling is weak as a result of a return of confidence in the franc, there is usually a decline of hoarding in France and other gold countries. Whenever sterling is firm as a result of a flight from the franc and other gold currencies, there is an increase of hoarding. This brings us to the main factor that affects the premium, viz. the supply and demand in the market.

The supply and demand is unable to affect the basic price of gold, which depends on the sterling-franc exchange rate.

So long as France is on the gold standard, substantial changes in supply and demand through an increase or decline of hoarding, or through whatever other reasons, can only affect the premium. For, if the changes are sufficiently pronounced, they cause the premium to rise above gold import point, or, as the case may be, they cause a discount to develop, in which case gold movements *from* Paris or *to* Paris would readjust the position.

APPENDIX IV

FORWARD DEALING IN GOLD

WE pointed out in Appendix I. that during the crisis a forward market has developed in gold. Strictly speaking, this development is not altogether new. In the East there has always been a limited and inadequate forward market for gold, both in India and China. In London itself there had already been forward transactions before the crisis. In particular during the period of weakness of sterling towards the end of 1930 and the beginning of 1931, the practice was adopted of buying the South African gold production before it had reached the London market. As soon as the gold left the Johannesburg refinery it was bought forward. The reason for this was the peculiar situation arising from the Bank of England's decision to pay out gold of standard fineness only and the decision of the Bank of France to accept gold of 0·996 fineness only. It was necessary, in consequence, to have the gold bars withdrawn from the Bank of England refined before delivering them to the Bank of France. As the refining facilities available both in London and Paris fell short of requirements, it was impossible to ship to Paris a sufficient amount of gold to offset the selling pressure on sterling. The result was a depreciation of sterling below gold export point. This again caused some uneasiness among French holders of sterling balances who sought to cover themselves by acquiring gold for later delivery. As the Bank of England itself was not prepared to undertake the forward sale of gold, they bought forward the South African gold output. When the peculiar situation came to an end early in 1931 through the decision of the Bank of France to accept in future bar gold of standard fineness, the practice of buying gold for forward delivery was also discontinued.

After the suspension of the gold standard in Great Britain,

regular forward dealing in gold gradually developed. The practice is not officially recognised, and when the bullion brokers fix the daily official price of gold they only transact business in gold for spot delivery. Unofficially, however, there is fairly active dealing in forward gold; there are days when several hundreds of thousands of pounds change hands.

Forward gold is always at a premium against spot gold, but the premium fluctuates within narrow limits: usually it is between 1s. and 1s. 2d. for three months and 2s. 2d. to 2s. 5d. for six months. At that rate it secures an adequate yield to holders of gold who are prepared to sell their holdings forward, allowing for the expenses attached to keeping gold deposited during three months. Those who possess facilities of their own for the purpose can earn over 3 per cent per annum on the capital engaged in such transactions.

Among the buyers of forward gold are speculators who expect sterling to depreciate and expect the price of gold to rise in consequence. It may be asked why such speculators do not buy forward francs or forward dollars instead of buying forward gold. The premium on forward francs is much lower than the premium on forward gold, while forward dollars can be acquired at a discount. If, in spite of this, they are prepared to pay the relatively high premium on gold, it is because in buying forward francs or dollars they expose themselves to the risk of a depreciation of those two currencies in terms of gold, in addition to the risk of an appreciation of sterling; while if they buy forward gold they are only exposed to the risk of appreciation of sterling. Another purpose for which gold is bought forward is to secure residents in the countries of the Gold Bloc against a devaluation of their national currencies. The same object can be achieved, of course, at a much lower cost by buying spot gold and keeping it on deposit in London. In many cases, however, those desirous of safeguarding themselves against a devaluation of their currencies are not in a position to immobilise their capital for some length of time; or possibly they earn a yield on their capital in excess of the cost of the forward gold operation. Let us suppose, for instance, that a Swiss capitalist wants to safeguard his capital, tied up in

Swiss trustee securities, against a depreciation of the Swiss franc. To that end, he has to sell Swiss francs forward, and at the same time buy gold forward for the same period. If, before the contracts mature, the franc depreciates in terms of gold, he will have the full benefit of the rise of gold in terms of Swiss francs. By merely selling Swiss francs forward against sterling, he might obtain the same profit, but he is exposed to the risk of a depreciation of sterling in terms of Swiss francs. If, however, the transaction is combined with a forward purchase of gold, then he is safeguarded against that risk.

Gold is also bought forward for the purpose of hedging operations by British speculators in Wall Street and other foreign markets. Needless to say, the hedging is far from watertight, for an appreciation of sterling and the fall in the sterling price of gold might easily inflict loss upon them.

Sellers of forward gold are, in the first place, holders of gold desirous of earning an interest; as the risk involved in selling forward gold is very small, provided that the deal is done with the right people, it is a profitable line of activity. Speculators who anticipate an appreciation of sterling also may find it more convenient to sell gold forward rather than contracting a short position in dollars or francs. Forward selling of gold is also used as a hedge against the depreciation of the dollar or franc by holders of American or French securities. Lastly, some holders of gold-mining shares who want to eliminate the exchange risk can do so by selling gold forward, even though in taking this course they also eliminate their chances of benefiting by a depreciation of sterling.

Another type of gold transaction that has developed recently, especially in France, is dealing in gold options. If a Frenchman fears a devaluation of the franc, one way of safeguarding himself against it is to buy an option for three or six months for the delivery of gold at the present selling price of the Bank of France. As most people in France are convinced that there will be no devaluation in the near future, such options can be bought at a very low price. The cost of such transactions is a little over 1½ per cent per annum.

APPENDIX V

LEGISLATION ON GOLD HOARDING

UNTIL 1928 hoarding of gold in Great Britain was free to everybody. The amount of gold British subjects or foreigners were entitled to hold was subject to no restriction. Even during the war, anyone withdrawing gold from the Bank was at liberty to hoard it, and was only prosecuted if he attempted to export it. It was not until 1928 that a restriction was imposed upon the unlimited hoarding of gold by British subjects. Without prohibiting such hoarding, the Currency and Bank Notes Act authorised the Bank of England to call in any amounts exceeding £10,000, against payment of its statutory buying price of 84s. 10d. per ounce of fine gold.

Clause 11 is the only existing text of legislation affecting private holdings of gold in this country. This clause is worded as follows:

"(1) With a view to the concentration of the gold reserves and to the securing of economy in the use of gold, the following provisions of this section shall have effect so long as subsection (1) of section one of the Gold Standard Act, 1925, remains in force.

"(2) Any person *in the United Kingdom* owning any gold coin or bullion to an amount exceeding ten thousand pounds in value shall, on being required so to do by notice in writing from the Bank, forthwith furnish to the Bank in writing particulars of the gold coin and bullion owned by that person, and shall, if so required by the Bank, sell to the Bank the whole or any part of the said coin or bullion, other than any part thereof which is *bona fide* held for immediate export or which is *bona fide* required for industrial purposes, on payment therefor by the Bank, in the case of coin, of the nominal value thereof, and in the case of bullion, at the rate fixed in section four of the Bank Charter Act, 1844."

APPENDIX VI—*continued*

WORLD GOLD PRODUCTION

(In Millions of Gold Pounds at 84/11½d. per Fine Ounce)

	Union of S. Africa	Canada	U.S.A.	U.S.S.R.	Rest of World	World	Percentage Annual Increase	British Empire	British Empire % of Total
	£m.	£m.	£m.	£m.	£m.	£m.	%	£m.	%
1913	37·4	3·4	18·3	8·3	30·0	97·4	—	59·4	61·0
1914	35·7	3·3	19·4	8·3	26·2	92·9	– 4·6	57·1	61·4
1915	38·6	3·9	20·8	6·5	27·9	97·7	+ 5·2	61·1	62·5
1916	39·5	4·0	19·0	6·2	26·5	95·2	– 2·6	60·1	63·2
1917	38·3	3·1	17·2	4·2	24·1	86·9	– 8·7	56·2	64·7
1918	35·8	3·0	14·1	2·8	23·7	79·4	– 8·6	51·5	64·8
1919	35·4	3·3	12·4	0·9	21·8	73·8	– 7·1	50·5	68·4
1920	34·7	3·2	10·5	0·2	19·9	68·5	– 7·2	48·2	70·3
1921	34·5	3·9	10·3	0·3	19·0	68·0	– 0·7	47·8	70·3
1922	29·8*	5·4	9·7	1·2	20·1	66·2	– 2·6	44·8	67·7
1923	38·9	5·2	10·3	1·9	20·1	76·4	+ 15·4	53·5	70·0
1924	40·7	6·5	10·4	2·5	19·2	79·3	+ 3·8	56·1	70·7
1925	40·8	7·4	9·9	2·9	18·6	79·6	+ 0·4	56·3	70·8
1926	42·3	7·5	9·5	3·8	18·7	81·8	+ 2·8	57·8	70·7
1927	43·0	7·9	9·0	3·4	18·2	81·5	– 0·4	58·8	72·2
1928	44·0	8·0	9·1	3·8	17·5	82·4	+ 1·1	59·6	72·3
1929	44·2	8·2	8·7	4·6	17·5	83·2	+ 1·0	59·9	72·0
1930	45·5	9·0	8·9	6·1	19·0	88·5	+ 6·4	62·1	70·2
1931	46·2	11·4	9·4	7·2	20·6	94·8	+ 7·1	66·1	69·7
1932	49·1	12·9	9·4	8·5	22·6	102·5	+ 8·1	71·8	70·0
1933 (est.)	46·9	12·4	9·1	8·5	25·1	102·0	– 0·5	70·2	68·9

* Output temporarily reduced by strike of white miners on Witwatersrand.

APPENDIX VIII—*continued*

Country	In Millions of Gold Dollars of the Original Weight and Fineness							
	1929	1930	1931		1932		1933	
	Dec.	Dec.	June	Dec.	June	Dec.	June	Dec.
Europe (excluding U.S.S.R.) . .	4,567	5,053	5,112	5,865	6,510	6,484	6,475	6,515
Albania . .	..	..	..	1	1	1	1	1
Germany . .	560	544	354	251	215	209	62	109
Austria . .	24	30	30	27	21	21	21	27
Belgium . .	163	191	200	354	357	361	372	380
Bulgaria . .	10	11	11	11	11	11	11	11
Denmark . .	46	46	46	39	36	36	36	36
Danzig . .	..	..	..	4	7	4	6	6
Spain . .	495	471	468	434	435	436	436	436
Estonia . .	2	2	2	2	3	4	5	5
Finland . .	8	8	8	8	8	8	8	8
France . .	1,631	2,099	2,211	2,683	3,217	3,257	3,183	3,015
Greece . .	8	7	6	11	7	8	14	24
Hungary . .	29	29	20	18	17	17	17	14
Italy . . .	273	279	283	296	298	307	356	373
Latvia . .	5	5	5	6	7	7	9	9
Lithuania . .	4	4	4	5	5	5	5	5
Norway . .	39	39	39	42	40	39	40	38
Netherlands .	180	171	200	357	394	415	309	371
Poland . .	79	63	64	67	54	56	53	53
Portugal . .	9	9	9	13	17	24	31	34
Roumania .	55	55	53	58	56	57	58	59
United Kingdom and Irish Free State .	711	722	800	590	666	587	927	933
Sweden . .	66	65	64	55	55	55	71	99
Switzerland .	115	138	162	453	503	477	361	386
Czechoslovakia	37	46	46	49	49	51	51	51
Yugoslavia .	18	19	27	31	31	31	32	32
Oceania . .	117	104	103	79	77	62	23	23
Australia . .	89	75	74	51	51	41	2	2
New Zealand .	28	29	29	28	26	21	21	21
Total .	10,406	11,055	11,391	11,393	11,456	..	11,968	12,040

APPENDIX VIII

MONETARY GOLD STOCKS

THE following table, extracted from the Statistical Year-Book of the League of Nations for 1933–1934, indicates the changes in the monetary gold stocks of the world during the crisis:

Country	In Millions of Gold Dollars of the Original Weight and Fineness							
	1929	1930	1931		1932		1933	
	Dec.	Dec.	June	Dec.	June	Dec.	June	Dec.
AFRICA . .	77	73	69	78	89	86	118	131
Algeria . .	8	8	8	8	8	8	8	8
Belgian Congo.	1	1	1	2	2	2	2	2
Egypt . .	19	20	21	21	33	33	33	33
Morocco . .	3	3	3	4	4	4	4	4
Union of South Africa . .	46	41	36	43	42	39	71	84
NORTH AMERICA	4,051	4,419	4,750	4,195	3,599	4,182	4,125	4,139
Canada . .	151	194	157	144	133	137	128	127
U.S.A. . .	3,900	4,225	4,593	4,051	3,466	4,045	3,997	4,012
CENTRAL AND SOUTH AMERICA	716	556	470	368	364	362	385	371
Argentine. .	405	411	349	252	248	248	248	238
Bolivia . .	5	2	2	5	5	5	4	4
Brazil . .	150	11	..	..	..	..	..	..
Chile . . .	8	8	8	12	12	10	11	12
Colombia . .	22	17	10	9	13	12	15	14
Ecuador . .	1	1	1	1	1	3	3	3
Mexico . .	8	5	5	2	2	4	22	18
Peru . . .	21	18	16	12	10	11	11	11
Uruguay . .	68	61	58	53	50	48	50	50
Venezuela .	18	15	15	15	15	15	15	15
Other countries	10	7	6	7	8	6	6	6
ASIA . . .	731	601	626	480	468	468	441	445
Straits Settlements . .	2	2	2	2	2	2	2	2
India . .	128	128	151	162	162	162	165	162
Neth. Indies .	56	56	46	45	42	42	42	44
Japan . .	542	412	424	234	214	213	212	212
Philippines .	3	3	3	10	11	12	12	13
Siam . .	..	..	..	23	28	28	..	..
Turkey . .	..	..	..	4	9	10	11	12
U.S.S.R. . .	147	249	261	328	349	..	401	416

The following table shows the amounts of gold produced or imported from India and China during 1933:

1933	Gold Production	Gold from India and China	Gold absorbed by Arts (estimated)	Net Total
	(Millions of Swiss Francs)			
1st quarter . .	650	253	-30	873
2nd " . .	645	221	-30	836
3rd " . .	668	194	-30	832
4th " . .	685	146	-30	801
	2648	814	-120	3342

APPENDIX VII

GOLD HOARDING STATISTICS

THE Bank for International Settlements has made a useful contribution to monetary statistics by the publication, in its Annual Report for 1933–1934, of its estimates of gold-hoarding during 1933. Although its figures are not complete—for instance, in the absence of information about the gold stock of the British Exchange Equalisation Account, this item has been omitted—they constitute, nevertheless, the most reliable statistical material on the subject.

The following table gives particulars of changes in the gold reserves of 50 countries every month during 1933, compared with the estimated amount of new gold that became available. The surplus or deficit represents the estimated amount of dishoarding or hoarding:

1933	Changes in Gold Reserves of U.S.A.	Changes in Reserves of 49 Other Countries	Total Changes for 50 Countries	Deducting Net Total of new Gold available	Dishoarding (+) or Hoarding (−)
	(Millions of Swiss Francs)				
January	+ 150	− 5	+ 145	− 270	− 125
February	− 1379	+425	− 954	− 270	− 1224
March	+ 560	+466	+1026	− 270	+ 756
April	+ 316	− 129	+ 187	− 270	− 83
May	+ 73	− 519	− 446	− 270	− 716
June	+ 31	− 161	− 130	− 270	− 400
July	+ 21	+430	+ 451	− 270	+ 181
August	+ 41	+265	+ 630	− 270	+ 36
September	+ 10	+265	+ 275	− 270	+ 5
October	..	+ 36	+ 36	− 270	− 234
November	+ 5	− 518	− 513	− 270	− 783
December	..	− 161	− 155	− 270	− 425
	− 172	+400	+ 228	− 3240	− 3012

APPENDIX IX

GOLD PRICES IN 1931–1934

The following table shows the highest and lowest market price of gold in London between August 1931 and September 1934:

	Highest		Lowest	
	s.	d.	s.	d.
1931				
August .	84	11½	84	10
September	114	9	84	10
October .	108	6	103	8
November	117	11	108	2
December	126	10	118	9
1932				
January .	122	9	117	11
February	120	9	118	5
March .	118	10	108	11
April .	113	5	108	4
May .	113	7	112	5
June .	114	8	112	2
July .	117	8	115	0
August .	119	3	117	0
September	119	5	117	11
October .	125	8	119	2
November	130	8	123	2½
December	130	0½	123	4½
1933				
January .	123	8	121	1½
February	122	0	119	9
March .	121	11½	118	11
April .	122	9	118	0
May .	124	8	122	5
June .	123	0	122	0
July .	124	10	122	4½
August .	129	7	124	0
September	133	9	127	7
October .	134	8	128	1
November	133	3	125	1½
December	127	0	124	8
1934				
January .	133	1	126	8
February	140	0	134	9
March .	137	2	135	5½
April .	135	11	134	3
May .	137	0½	135	10
June .	138	2½	137	1½
July .	138	0½	137	5
August .	140	11½	137	10
September	141	7	140	3½
For 1931 .	126	10	84	10
For 1932 .	130	8	108	4
For 1933 .	134	8	118	0
For 1934 (Jan.-Sept.)	141	7	126	8